simply
small
groups

simply small groups

[
Differentiating
Literacy Learning
in Any Setting
]

resources.corwin.com/simplysmallgroups

debbie diller

CORWIN Literacy

For information:

Corwin
A SAGE Company
2455 Teller Road
Thousand Oaks, California 91320
(800) 233-9936
www.corwin.com

SAGE Publications Ltd.
1 Oliver's Yard
55 City Road
London EC1Y 1SP
United Kingdom

SAGE Publications India Pvt. Ltd.
B 1/I 1 Mohan Cooperative Industrial Area
Mathura Road, New Delhi 110 044
India

SAGE Publications Asia-Pacific Pte. Ltd.
18 Cross Street #10–10/11/12
China Square Central
Singapore 048423

President: Mike Soules
Associate Vice President and
    Editorial Director: Monica Eckman
Executive Editor: Tori Mello Bachman
Associate Content Development Editor:
    Sharon Wu
Editorial Assistant: Nancy Chung
Production Editor: Melanie Birdsall
Copy Editor: Heather Kerrigan
Typesetter: Integra
Proofreader: Lawrence W. Baker
Cover Designer: Gail Buschman
Marketing Manager: Margaret O'Connor

Library of Congress Cataloging-in-Publication Data

Names: Diller, Debbie, author.
Title: Simply small groups : differentiating literacy learning in any
    setting / Debbie Diller.
Description: Thousand Oaks, California : Corwin Press, Inc., [2022] |
    Series: Corwin literacy
Identifiers: LCCN 2021027035 | ISBN 9781071847060 (paperback) |
    ISBN 9781071855430 (adobe pdf)
Subjects: LCSH: Group reading. | Individualized instruction. | Group work
    in education. | Small groups.
Classification: LCC LC6615 .D55 2022 | DDC 372.41/62--dc23
    LC record available at https://lccn.loc.gov/2021027035

Printed in the United States of America

This book is printed on acid-free paper.

21 22 23 24 25 10 9 8 7 6 5 4 3 2 1

Contents

online resources

Visit the companion website at
resources.corwin.com/simplysmallgroups
for downloadable resources.

Dear Reader,

As a pandemic swept our world, the educational landscape was disrupted. What we'd done in the past changed overnight. Teachers faced many difficult questions: Which lessons should I record? What should I teach live? How can I engage and motivate my students? How can I help students who read at a wide variety of levels?

As we move through this great crisis and into whatever comes next, let's ask other questions: What do I believe about learning? What do I know from my experience that I can build on?

I believe that all children *can* learn; all children *want* to learn; all children *do* learn. To get the most from our time together, we must all *be* learners— educators and students alike. I believe that one way to help each other learn is by working together in small groups. No matter if we are in a brick-and-mortar building or if we are teaching online from our kitchens, I believe that what matters most is relationships! And small groups are one of the best ways to establish connections and build relationships with and among our students.

In this book, we will explore different types of small groups for literacy. We will look at groups focused on building oral language, groups for emergent readers who are learning to look at print, small groups for writing, and groups for kids who are learning to apply phonics. We will examine guided reading groups and book clubs, as well as inquiry groups and writing groups.

Because most classrooms have students in a wide range of different reading levels, I've arranged this book by developmental stages to make it simple for you to use. You'll find sections focused on *emergent readers*— those students just learning about sounds and letters—as well as *early readers*—children who are breaking the phonetic code as they read to comprehend. There's a section focused on *transitional readers*—students who are reading lengthier books but still learning new words and developing fluency and comprehension. And there's another focused on *fluent readers*—kids who can often decode many words but are expanding their view of the world as they explore new genres, study word morphology, and comprehend more deeply through text analysis.

I've included characteristics for each stage of literacy learning to help you zero in on the best work to engage children where they are, regardless of grade level, and help them to progress to the next stage. There are charts to simplify what to focus on at each reading stage and connected phonological awareness and phonics, fluency, vocabulary, and comprehension teaching tips. There are sample lesson plans and ideas for online learning. The goal is to support you as much as possible as you support students who are moving through the full range of reading development.

Your school might use a leveling system, such as Fountas and Pinnell, Scholastic, DRA, Reading A–Z, or Lexile reading levels. Or you may have other schoolwide assessments used to collect data. You may be teaching face-to-face in a classroom; some of your students may be learning in an online setting. You may be providing synchronous and/or asynchronous instruction. Regardless of where you are, you can benefit from and tailor the information in this book to match your needs.

I encourage you to embrace a growth mindset as you use this book to plan and teach in small groups. Instead of thinking about closing learning gaps, let's build on students' strengths. Honor what each child brings to small group time and help them work toward meeting small but steady reading growth goals. Meet with your children regularly in small groups. Listen and learn alongside them. I believe that if we pay attention to what students know and what they are interested in *and* we understand literacy development, we will better serve our children as we guide them to read, write, and think in deeper ways.

Yours in learning,

Debbie

#simplystations

@debbie.diller
(Instagram)

https://www
.facebook.com/
dillerdebbie
(Facebook)

@debbiediller
(Twitter)

www.debbiediller
.com
(website)

1

Small Group Basics

Today more than ever, small group literacy instruction is needed in our class-rooms! Regardless of your instructional setting—face-to-face, completely online, hybrid, simultaneous, or anything else—our students need the relation-ships that are best forged in small groups. Small groups provide a safe place for kids to learn together with the support of a teacher and their peers.

In your classroom you may have some children who are just learning sounds and letters, while others are reading at grade-level standard. There may be students advancing into levels beyond those typically read at your grade level. You may have students learning a new language. How do you differentiate to guide learners at so many different stages? Small groups!

In this section, you will find answers to many questions you may have about small group time. Read through it to find general information on small group teaching. Then use the other sections of this book to pinpoint what you might do in those small groups to differentiate instruction for students at various reading levels. Sections 2–5 each focus on a different stage of reading development, from emergent through early, transitional, and fluent stages.

To keep things simple, the guided reading levels in this book are based on the Fountas and Pinnell (F&P) system, which has been in use since the 1990s in North America. You'll find information about this and other leveling systems (e.g., Lexile, Reading A to Z, and DRA2) in Section 6 and in the online compan-ion at **resources.corwin.com/simplysmallgroups**. This reference, A Quick Look at Reading Levels, can help you think about differentiation as you use the resources in this book.

Regardless of the leveling system you use, the strategies and tools in this book are based on a continuum of development. Students will move between devel-opmental stages across this continuum. In fact, our goal is to accelerate young readers across this continuum by differentiating in small groups. Please find the reading behaviors that match your students and plan from there.

Section 6 includes a chart, A Simple Look at Language Acquisition, which you can also download and print from the online companion, **resources .corwin.com/simplysmallgroups**. Use this chart along with tips for support-ing English language learners (EL tips) found throughout this book to plan for differentiation according to language levels.

> Children who are learning online need to build relationships with you and their peers. They may not have siblings or other kids to interact with daily. This makes small group time even more critical for social skills and literacy development.

Small Group Basics

Why Are Small Groups Important for Literacy Learning?

I believe we make time for what we value the most. If we can articulate the importance of small group reading instruction, we will be more likely to include this differentiated time for students daily. The following list was generated by a group of teachers. They affirm that small group instruction:

ONLINE LEARNING TIP: Communicate expectations with students and or caregivers so children are present and prepared for small group instruction.

- Accelerates children's reading and writing growth, starting where they are

- Builds relationships between students and the teacher

- Encourages kids to feel safe to take risks and try new things as readers, writers, and thinkers

- Helps students feel like they belong at school (or online)

- Allows kids to practice social skills with just a few others at a time

- Gives teachers the opportunity to more carefully observe student learning

- Provides opportunity for children to get immediate feedback

- Increases participation because there are fewer kids in a small group

- Uses data to target specific student needs

- Engages kids in individualized and differentiated instruction

- Gives opportunities to practice talking to students learning a new language

ONLINE LEARNING TIP: Because it is difficult to differentiate whole group or asynchronous tasks during virtual instruction, small group instruction is critical for online learners.

What Is the Purpose of Small Group Literacy Instruction?

Small group is a time to work closely with students, a time to get to know them and build on their strengths and interests. It is a time to listen, learn, and develop relationships. By working with just a few kids at a time, you can establish a safe, trusting classroom environment—and this holds true whether you're teaching in person, online, or in any combination of the two.

The purpose of small group instruction is to work with students where they are along the continuum and help them grow. Instead of having each small group work on the same thing you've taught in whole group (according to your district scope and sequence), use small group time to differentiate—provide instruction that matches your students and will help them accelerate.

For example, even if you're teaching inference in whole group according to your curriculum goals, you may still have some kids stuck on short vowels; others might need help decoding words with long vowel patterns. Inference is not the immediate need of all students in your room, even if your data show that students didn't do well with this skill on the weekly assessment or end-of-unit test. If kids can't read the words, how can they possibly infer? Continue to work with inference as you read aloud and think aloud in whole class. But during small group, focus on short vowels, long vowel patterns, or whatever kids need in their different groups.

ONLINE LEARNING TIP: Use a screen recording tool as you model how to access online learning platforms and apps. Share your screen and move slowly step-by-step in live meetings. Post videos online for new families to view throughout the year.

EL TIP: Multilingual students will benefit by working in small groups where they can develop social and academic language and feel supported. These students are learning content *and* language, so positive reinforcement and a celebratory vibe are important.

Be flexible and customize small groups to meet a variety of purposes that match the needs of the children in your care. Consider what you know about reading development (using tools from this book) to target the specific areas that will help students accelerate as readers, writers, and thinkers. When planning small group time, think less about standards and more about students and what they *can* do. Build from where your kids are.

Consider these small group options and related purposes as you work with diverse learners in your classroom. (A printable labeled Types of Small Groups and Who Will Be in Each is available in the online companion, **resources .corwin.com/simplysmallgroups**.)

During small group time, you can encourage students who are not reading and writing on grade level to build from things they *can* do.

Types of Small Groups

TYPE OF SMALL GROUP	DEVELOPMENTAL STAGE	PURPOSE
Oral language group	Emergent readers and newcomers to a language	• Develop language through speaking (e.g., longer sentences, vocabulary development, oral grammar usage)
Sound and letter learning group	Emergent readers	• Build phonological awareness (sound work) • Learn sounds, letter names, and letter formation
Shared reading group	Emergent readers	• Develop print awareness (e.g., high-frequency words, left to right, one to one)
Guided reading group	Emergent, early, and transitional readers	• Support students where they are (using developmental reading levels) and guide their reading practice
Word study group	All stages	• Learn phonics, spelling, and vocabulary that match development (e.g., emergent: kids' names, CVC work; early: high-frequency words and phonics; transitional: phonics patterns and vocabulary; fluent: morphology)
Writing group	All stages	• Connect reading to writing; write responses • Build a love of writing and know their voice is valued • Improve writing craft and conventions at children's development level
Book club	Transitional and fluent readers	• Deepen comprehension • Create a community of fluent, avid readers
Inquiry group	Fluent readers	• Independently and collaboratively investigate to find answers to questions students have • Use findings to take actionable steps

As you work with a wide variety of learners in your classroom, pay attention to their needs in small group. If you notice that kids aren't progressing, seek out additional resources or help that your school staff might provide. Documenting student progress can help kids get the special support they may need in addition to what you're doing.

ONLINE LEARNING TIP: Place links to online meetings and digital resources in the shared schedule. Recommend that caregivers create and post a (flexible) daily schedule in their child's learning space to help them know what to expect. A small clock can be helpful, too.

How Do Small Groups Fit Into the Literacy Block?

Most classroom schedules include time for whole group, small group, partner work, and one-on-one time daily. Small group is an important time of the day—an essential component no matter if you teach face-to-face, online, hybrid, or in any other setting. What follows are some sample schedules to show where small group instruction fits in the day. Be flexible and create a schedule that works for you.

SAMPLE PRIMARY SCHEDULE for LITERACY

8:00–8:10	Morning Meeting (community building time)
8:10–8:25	Whole Group Lesson for Modeling Using Interactive Read Aloud
8:25–8:45	Small Group and Literacy Stations (round one)
8:45–9:05	Small Group and Literacy Stations (round two)
9:05–9:15	Reflection Time for Stations and Small Group
9:15–9:20	Brain Break
9:20–9:35	Whole Group Lesson for Modeling Using Shared Reading and Word Study
9:35–9:55	Whole Class Independent Reading Time (teacher confers 1:1 or may meet with a third small group)
9:55–10:05	Whole Group Lesson for Modeling Writing
10:05–10:30	Whole Class Independent Writing Time (teacher confers with students 1:1 or may meet with a small group for writing)
10:30–10:40	Sharing/Reflection Time for Writing

SAMPLE INTERMEDIATE SCHEDULE for LITERACY

8:00–8:10	Morning Meeting (community building time; students do book talks/share what they're reading)
8:10–8:25	Whole Group Lesson for Modeling Using Interactive Read Aloud or Shared Reading Integrating Word Study/Vocabulary
8:25–8:45	Whole Class Independent Reading Time (teacher confers 1:1 or may meet with a small group for reading)
8:45–9:05	Small Groups, including Book Clubs and Inquiry Groups with Literacy Stations (some teachers do another twenty-minute round of small group and stations if schedules allow)
9:05–9:15	Whole Group Lesson for Modeling Writing
9:15–9:40	Whole Class Independent Writing Time (teacher confers with students 1:1 or may meet with a small group for writing)
9:40–9:50	Reflection Time for Reading and Writing

ONLINE LEARNING TIP: Plan for live small groups daily at consistent times. Don't record small group lessons for kids to watch. The purpose of online small groups is for interaction and relationship building.

How Does Whole Group Literacy Instruction Relate to Small Group Instruction?

ONLINE LEARNING TIP: Record whole group lessons in case someone is absent or needs to review so they can go back and watch it.

Whole group is a time to model and expose everyone in your class to grade-level text and standards even if students aren't reading at grade level. During whole group instruction, read aloud engaging text to your class. Think aloud as you model how to make predictions and connections, ask and answer questions, and infer or think beyond the text. Teach grade-level phonics lessons (and related phonemic awareness) to your class using a systematic program.

Write aloud in front of your class during whole group. Show how you come up with writing ideas, compose pieces with your children watching and helping, and reread your writing, thinking aloud about other words you might use or parts you forgot to include. It's important for children to learn that making mistakes and not getting everything perfect are part of the process. Provide time for independent reading and writing for your whole class, too. As students read and write, walk around the room and confer with individuals. Check in to see what kids are reading and writing. Listen to some read, watch some write, invite a few to read a bit to you, and ask questions and offer encouragement and gentle nudges.

Teach well in whole group and observe during independent time before moving into small groups. Your observations and data inform what each child needs to focus on. During small group time, model with and expect students to use the same academic vocabulary you instructed with. Use conversation cards—speech bubbles that guide student discussion—as prompts and scaffolds. (You'll find these in my Simply Stations series and references in this book.)

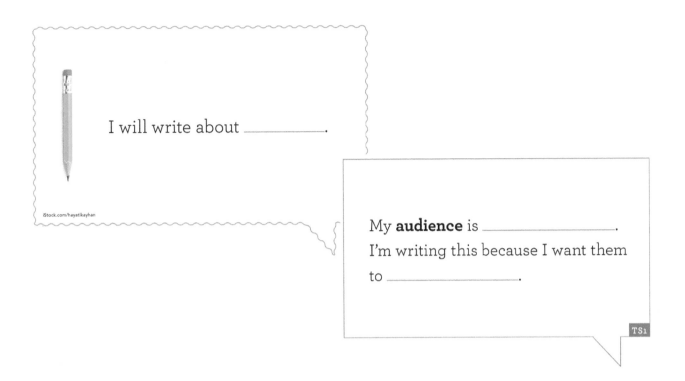

I will write about _____.

My **audience** is _____.
I'm writing this because I want them to _____.

TS1

Over time, move graphic organizers you've taught with in whole group to small group as well to support learning. For example, if kids are working with character traits in small group, provide the circle map you've modeled with previously in whole group to help readers keep track of their thinking about characters. Allow students to use the tools that best help them comprehend. One size does not fit all.

What About the Small Group Lessons That Come With Our Reading Program?

Your school may use a reading program that includes lessons for phonics and read-aloud. It may have related writing, spelling, and grammar lessons, too. Most likely, leveled text for small group instruction will be provided. These books and online resources can be useful, but you may need something more. Just because a text is labeled "below-level reader" doesn't guarantee that it will meet the needs of your students who are not reading where your school expects them to be at a given time. You may be a second- or third-grade teacher with students reading at emergent levels. The small group texts that accompany your grade-level materials most likely won't reach back that far.

Use what you know about your students and their development along with ideas from this book and the reading materials you can find at your school. Give yourself permission to borrow from other grade levels, if needed, and work with others to plan to meet the needs of your students in small group instruction.

ONLINE LEARNING TIP: Make short videos for families modeling how to work with students on key reading behaviors (e.g., how to prompt children to use word parts when decoding rather than telling kids the word).

What Is the Ideal Number of Students in Each Group? How Many Groups Should I Form?

Groups of about three to five students usually work best, depending on what kids need. Sometimes you might have only two children in a group, especially if those students need something totally different from the rest of the class. Or sometimes kids need more support and develop confidence faster in a very small group.

Occasionally there may be five or six children in a group, particularly if the students need just a little bit of support from you. But if all your groups are this large, you may not be able to give students the individualized support you'd like.

Try to make your groups small enough so that nobody can hide! It's not necessary to try to make all groups the same size. This isn't a simple division problem. Remember, groups are based on student needs, not numbers.

I've found that most teachers can manage a total of four or five groups. If you form more than that, you may have trouble keeping up with them. These groups should be fluid and change throughout the school year. Students who start the year in one group may work with different students over time in small groups. Consider flexibly regrouping students among teachers at your grade level to meet students' needs, especially if you only have one child with needs very different from the rest of your class.

How Much Time Should I Allow for Small Group Instruction?

In kindergarten most small groups last from ten to fifteen minutes, depending on what students are working on. Meet with your youngest learners for short periods of time to keep interest and engagement high. Students in first and second grade might meet for about twenty minutes each. By third and fourth grade, the groups might last for twenty to twenty-five minutes.

If students need extra help, don't keep them longer! See their group more often or meet with them one-on-one during independent reading time. Keep small groups short and focused. Students may take more away and end on a note of success.

Instead of trying to fit everything you can think of into a lesson, focus on one thing that you want kids to be able to do well by the end of that small group meeting. Stick with the same focus for multiple meetings and watch the benefits grow.

ONLINE LEARNING TIP: Provide tech support videos for students and caregivers to refer to at any time. This can maximize instruction time.

How Often Should I Meet With Each Group?

Every week include every child in some type of small group instruction. It's not necessary to meet with every group every day (unless you have another adult in the room and you both work with several groups). There just aren't enough minutes in the day to plan for and implement that many small group lessons!

Try to work with two small groups in a row for literacy. Then schedule a whole group activity or brain break. If you want to meet with a third literacy group, have it after this short break.

Meet with students who need more support more often. I like to create a schedule with sticky notes or a whiteboard for a week or two at a time. Post this schedule near your small group table where you can easily refer to and rearrange it as needed. The photo shows an example.

ONLINE LEARNING TIP: Some teachers meet face-to-face with students several days a week and online groups on other days. If you have a hybrid setting, you might meet with small groups on days kids are in the building.

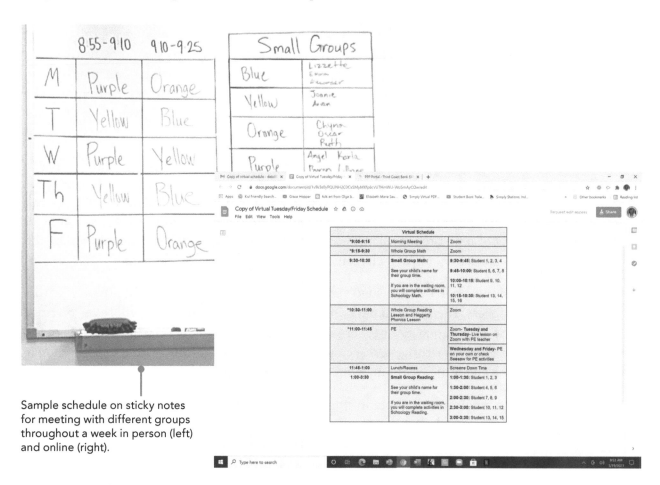

Sample schedule on sticky notes for meeting with different groups throughout a week in person (left) and online (right).

Some types of groups will meet more independently of the teacher. For example, book clubs for fluent readers may meet one or two times a week without you. Occasionally, you'll want to visit these groups to provide support and check on student progress. Similarly, inquiry groups for fluent readers may need your help periodically, but you won't need to meet with them as regularly as a guided reading group. (Read more about these groups in Section 5.) Use the printable forms online to plan for when you will meet with which groups over a week or two at a time.

How Often Should Small Groups Change?

Once you have formed a small group, meet with those students until the group no longer serves their needs. For example, over time you may notice that the leveled texts a group is reading become too easy for a student. So advance that child to a group reading at the appropriate level. Or, a few kids may not be progressing as quickly as the rest of their small group, so you move those students into a group that better matches their needs and will help them feel successful.

Some students may be in more than one group. For example, a child at the early reading stage may decode one-syllable words well but needs support in reading more fluently. Work with that student in a group at a slightly lower level to build fluency and confidence with text that is a bit easier. And also place that child in a second group that provides opportunities to grow in phonics skill at a slightly higher level.

Look at your groups every two to three weeks and make changes based on what you're noticing about each child's progress. The groups should be flexible. But don't worry if a group of students stays together for a while. Consider instead their learning growth. If kids aren't making progress in their groups, make changes in what you're doing and what they're reading in that small group time.

How Long Will It Take Me to Prepare for Small Groups?

Anything worth doing takes preparation—training for a race, making a fresh salad, painting a wall. And small group time is no exception. Having a plan for each small group will make things run smoothly and your students will be the benefactors. Make a plan, and then prepare to be flexible with it.

In this book I've provided simple-to-use planning templates to streamline this process. Having your data organized and at your fingertips will save you time, too. (See suggestions for creating a small group folder on page 19). Look at the reading or writing levels of your students to determine groups, then choose the matching planning form, select a focus and a text, and write a brief plan.

To maximize time planning for small groups, follow these steps. A printable chart is included in the online companion for you to keep at your fingertips while planning (**resources.corwin.com/simplysmallgroups**).

HOW to PLAN a SMALL GROUP LESSON

1. **Form a group** based on your data.

2. **Choose a focus** for multiple lessons. Use the corresponding Key Reading Behaviors chart.

3. **Choose *several* texts** that match that focus. Look in your classroom resources, school library, or book room. If you

---

can't find the kinds of books you need, ask administrators for help. Your school may need to purchase texts that match your students. Or you may need to borrow from other grade levels.

4. **Arrange** the three or four books you've selected in order from easiest to most challenging.

5. **Start** with the easiest book to build student success.

6. **Read** the book, and then **write a plan** to go with it.

7. **Adapt** the plan to write another lesson using the next book, and so on.

ONLINE LEARNING TIP: Use the same process described in the box to the left but find online texts for your students to read in small group.

Four related books arranged from easier to more difficult at Level A. The teacher will plan four lessons with the same focus: working with the high-frequency word *we*.

How Do I Get My Students Excited About Small Group Time?

Enthusiasm is contagious! If you are excited about meeting with your students in small group, they will be, too. An upper-grade teacher told me his kids thought small group was VIP time, because that's how he treated it.

Don't tell students they must meet with you because they need extra help. Instead, invite kids to your group for learning time. Tell them that you have selected them to work with you to learn new stuff together. You might post a schedule for which group meets on which day with group member names on it. When kids know what to expect, it relieves stress.

ONLINE LEARNING TIP: Children learning online crave connection with you and other students. Belonging to a small group gives kids a chance to get to know you and just a few other students at a time.

What Does the Rest of the Class Do During Small Groups?

The rest of your class should be engaged in meaningful work while you meet with a small group. I recommend using literacy stations—small, defined spaces (portable or stationary) where students practice with a partner. Students work together on things they *can* do, using familiar materials and tasks to practice reading, writing, listening, speaking, and/or working with words. Children use previously taught academic vocabulary as they engage in purposeful work that has been modeled previously in whole or small group instruction.

Starting the first week of school, begin introducing independent reading and partner reading in whole group. These will become your first literacy stations. Continue to teach whole group routines during the first four to six weeks of school where kids can work with partners. Layer new stations into the class rotation as you teach. For example, as you teach kids to self-select books and read independently with a purpose, they can do this same work at an Independent Reading station. Likewise, after you've modeled how to make connections to text read or heard, students can begin making connections as they listen to stories and information at a Listening and Speaking station. What happens in whole and small group flows into stations practice.

See my Simply Stations series for detailed support on how to set up, introduce, and sustain a variety of literacy stations. There is a book on each station—Independent Reading, Partner Reading, Listening and Speaking, Writing, and Poetry, to name a few. Each book includes step-by-step instructions for launching and maintaining the station, whole group lesson plans to introduce and support partner work, printable teacher and student tools, and real classroom photos so you can see the possibilities firsthand. The QR code in the margin takes you to a sample from *Simply Stations: Independent Reading*.

At some grade levels children may also be meeting in student-led small groups as well as literacy stations. See Section 5 of this book for ideas on book clubs, inquiry groups, and writing groups for fluent readers.

Students read and respond to books at an Independent Reading station.

Photo by Matthew Rood.

A pair of children listen and retell at the Listening and Speaking station.

A pair of children write stories at these Writing stations.

Two kids enjoy a book together at a Partner Reading station.

WANT to TRY LITERACY STATIONS ONLINE?

You might create a six-grid table with a Google Slide in each space that represents a station. Students click on the cell with a link that takes them to the station work they will do. Or use collaborative Google Slides. If you can use breakout rooms, have kids meet with a partner there to work together. They can share a Google Doc to type what they're learning. If you have younger students, a family member might work with them as a partner.

Google Slides represent literacy stations students will work at in an online classroom.

How Do I Minimize Interruptions?

During small group time, you'll want to prevent interruptions. Be proactive by taking these simple steps *before* starting small group. You'll find a printable Checklist to Prevent Small Group Interruptions chart in the online companion (**resources.corwin.com/simplysmallgroups**).

ONLINE LEARNING TIP: Online interruptions may take the form of poor internet connections. Keep your device hardwired, if possible, to avoid trouble on your end. And reinforce to children that if their internet drops out, they can quietly re-enter.

1. Teach routines well, beginning the first day of school. Set up a classroom system for expectations (e.g., bathroom procedures, Kleenex use, sharpening pencils), so kids can learn to manage these things without your direction.

2. Be sure you've taught and modeled routines and expectations in whole group, so children are working with *familiar* materials and tasks at literacy stations. Introduce stations, one at a time, and establish clear expectations for students practicing independently of you during small group time.

3. Don't start small group too early in the school year. Use the first few weeks of school to assess students and monitor their literacy stations to establish a strong foundation.

4. Use a physical object to remind children that small group is a protected time and not to be interrupted. Some teachers wear a funny hat or a sparkling tiara during small group as a visual

reminder. Others put a stop sign on their small group table as a visible "no interrupting" signal.

5. Set a large digital timer so students know how many minutes are left in the rotation. This can help them understand when to talk with you (between groups).

6. Don't give warnings! Use one strike and you're out. If kids aren't following expectations at literacy stations, have them sit quietly in a chair near your small group table and just watch until you can confer with them privately. They can return to their station when you know they understand what to do.

7. Establish expectations for noise so you and your students can focus at the small group table. Have a pre-taught signal (like a bell or chime) to get their attention if it gets too loud. Ask them why you stopped (it was too loud) and what needs to be done (turn down their volume). Then quickly resume your small group.

8. You might place a dry erase board near your small group table where kids can write you a quick note during stations if needed. Respond to these inquiries *between* groups.

9. Have a brief reflection time after stations (or between them early in the year) to provide paperless accountability and help students remember stations expectations.

ONLINE LEARNING TIP: Keep your phone handy during small groups online. If you work with young learners who need more support during small group, allow their adults to message you if questions arise about the group's activity.

A digital timer sets clear expectations for the rest of the class during small group time: *Don't interrupt small group. There are _____ more minutes for you to work without my help.*

Getting Started With Small Groups

First, get to know your students. Listen to them, read with them, and find out what they are interested in and what they can do. Then use what you've learned to form small groups. Look at children's reading and language development so you can plan instruction and opportunity that helps them grow. Finally, create a system for organizing this information to help you work efficiently and effectively. Invest the time to do this well before starting small group instruction. You'll build a strong foundation for small group that will help you and your students be successful all year long.

How Do I Assess My Students?

Use whatever data collection system your school has in place for literacy. This will most likely include phonological awareness and letter identification tasks (for young learners), phonics screeners, fluency assessments, and comprehension tests. There are screeners to determine the level of English language proficiency of the multilingual learners in your care. Some assessments may be administered on a device; for others, you will sit beside individual kids and take notes. Here are suggestions that may help:

- *Be sure to listen to every student read!* Go beyond computer-generated data, especially with younger students. Sometimes they just hit buttons and guess correctly. Or they don't understand the assessment tasks and score lower than they should.

- If you have children who aren't reading yet, have them use a familiar book to tell you the story. Note their oral language development and what they understand about print. Do they speak in sentences, use advanced vocabulary, include details?

- Some schools use leveled reading systems, such as the Developmental Reading Assessment (DRA) or the F&P Benchmark Assessment System. If you don't have something like this, use books from your grade-level reading program as a benchmark. Jot down decoding errors to help you analyze what children know and what they confuse. Make notes about their oral reading fluency (e.g., smooth, phrased, choppy). Have a conversation with them about what they read. Did they comprehend on the surface, deeply, or not at all?

- Look at students' reading *and* writing. Give kindergartners blank paper. Have them draw a picture and write something about themselves, including their name. Ask students in first through fourth grade to write you a letter or note introducing themselves. They can tell you about their likes and dislikes, their families, their pets, etc.

- Use children's writing as a benchmark assessment to show you what they understand about letters and words. Is their writing clear, organized, or a jumbled mess? You might sort their writing into four piles—hard to understand or indecipherable, rudimentary skills in place, pretty good communication, excellent writing for this age level—to use when forming small groups.

EL TIP: Remember that children learning English may have tremendous knowledge and skill but may struggle to demonstrate it because of language barriers. Getting to know them through conversation, looking at pictures, and listening in small group is key.

TIPS for ASSESSING STUDENTS ONLINE

- When assessing students online, be sure children (and caregivers) have clear instructions and easy-to-access links to assessments ahead of time.

- Ask students to show up early and come prepared.

- Keep channels of communication open between you and your families in case questions or problems arise.

- Plan for more time than you think online assessments will take to administer. If things don't go well (e.g., screaming babies in the background, adults giving answers), do the best you can.

- Ask students to keep cameras on during the assessment to determine how much help they are receiving at home.

- You might meet with caregivers *before* giving assessments. Email and text the information, too. Help adults understand that if they tell kids the answers, you won't really know what the student can do!

How Do I Form Small Groups?

Often the simplest solutions are the low-tech ones, regardless of whether you're teaching online or in person. All you need is a laminated folder and some small sticky notes to begin. Here are some simple steps to use when forming small groups:

1. Look at all your data. Input information on a spreadsheet (probably provided by your school) so you can look at your whole class at once.

2. Determine which students are emergent readers, early readers, transitional readers, and fluent readers. Use the How to Determine

the Child's Developmental Reading Level chart in the online companion for help. You might highlight emergent readers in one color and students in the transitional stage in another and so on to give you a snapshot of your class.

3. Use a folder to form your groups. (A brightly colored or patterned file folder will make it easy to find!)

Front of small group folder for forming groups

4. Open the file folder and divide the inside of it into four sections, as shown in the photos on the facing page. (If you have a fifth group, use the back of the folder.) Laminate your folder to make it dry erasable.

5. Write each child's name on a small sticky note tape flag or tab (so they all fit on one folder).

6. Place the names into groups based on what you've learned about your students from your assessment information. Think about forming groups to meet the needs of your children. You might ask yourself these questions:

   ○ What developmental reading stage is this child in? (Put kids in the same stage together so you can focus on working where they are and where they need to move next.)

   ○ What is the student's instructional reading level? (Group children reading at a similar level so they can read and discuss a book together with just a bit of teacher support. It's okay to put kids together that read at similar levels, like Levels H and I, instead of forming a separate group for each reading level.)

   ○ What can this child do as a reader? As a writer? As a speaker? (Place students in groups where you can build on their strengths.)

   ○ Is this learner's writing level as strong as their reading level? (Form some groups focused on writing as well as reading.)

   ○ What is this student interested in reading or learning about? (Form groups of fluent readers for book clubs, inquiry groups, or writing groups this way.)

   ○ What is the child's level of language development? (Consider the needs of students who are learning English as a new language, too.)

7. When you have all your sticky note flags sorted into groups, take another look. Do you have too many kids in one group? Are there students who might need a smaller group? Have you formed more groups than you can manage? Then label each group with the developmental stage kids are in (pre-emergent, emergent, early, transitional, or fluent). See the photo that follows for an example.

Children's names are written on sticky tabs and sorted into groups based on developmental reading stages.

8. Finally, look at the Key Reading Behaviors chart (in the online companion) that matches the developmental stage of each group. Print and cut out the strip that matches where each group is. Attach it to your folder with Velcro dots or paper clips as shown below. Then choose a focus based on what you notice that each group needs to accelerate. If you laminate the strips, you can circle the focus with a dry erase marker.

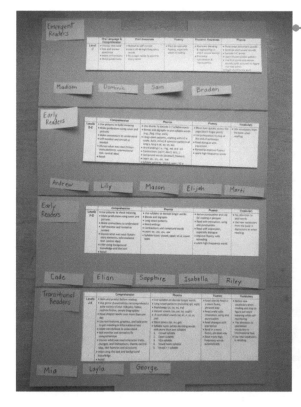

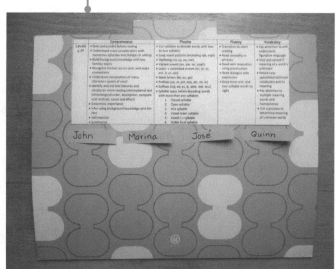

Small groups folder with matching key reading behaviors strips added for each group. The fifth group is on the back of the file folder.

ONLINE LEARNING TIP: Use a similar system for online learning groups, such as a Google Doc or a Padlet. With a Google Form, you can answer questions about each student and see data in a spreadsheet.

You might have two groups at the same level but working on different skills. For example, one group reading at emergent Level B might be working on high-frequency words, while another group at the same level is focused on starting CVC work. Watch what students *can* do and adjust the focus accordingly.

Be prepared to move kids into different groups based on what you notice when you work with them. And remember that you might have some students who work in more than one group depending on their needs. For example, you may have a child who is in a group with transitional readers at Level L, focusing on understanding point of view, and is also in a group with transitional readers at Level K to practice reading in a more fluent, phrased way.

How Do I Keep Track of It All?

Many teachers use some sort of binder or notebook to keep track of their small groups. There are many ways to set this up, but the key is to keep things organized in a way that fits your needs. While there is no one, perfect way, here are some suggestions for organizing your binder:

- Have a section marked with a colored divider for each small group.

- Consider using dividers with pockets. You can place materials needed in the pocket. Or use the pockets to store index cards labeled with kids' names for anecdotal notes.

- Write lesson plans, three-hole punch them, and place them in the section matching that group.

- Clean out your notebook every six weeks so it doesn't become unmanageable.

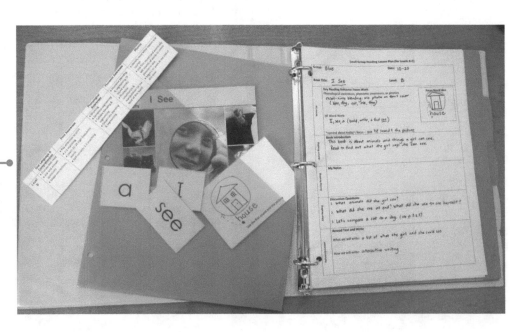

Small group binder has colored dividers with pockets for each group.

You might also use magazine file boxes or plastic bins for storing materials needed. This will be helpful even if you are teaching online from your home office. Here are some ways you can use containers for organizing:

- Store file folders for each student in a magazine file box. Keep running records or other data sheets in these folders.

- Place materials for this week's lessons in a box within arm's reach.

- Label bins with materials grouped by category (e.g., concepts about print [CAP], rhyming, phonemic awareness, letter ID) for young learners.

Portable vertical file folder box holds small group reading materials and student data files.

Labeled bins in a kindergarten classroom hold small group teaching materials for emergent readers.

Post a schedule for small groups on a wall by your small group teaching area. Use this for quick reference. It will help you and your students know when you are meeting with each group. Using a dry erase board or sticky notes will make this a flexible space. The photos show examples from actual classrooms.

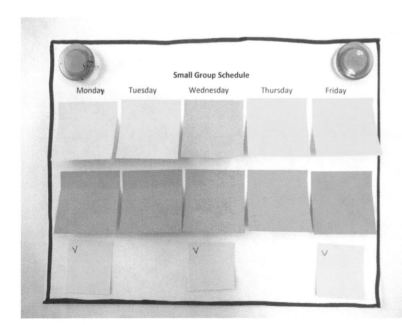

Sticky notes are used to post the week's small group schedule. A small "v" indicates virtual groups.

[What Are *the* Essential Materials?]

Set up a small group area with all your materials at your fingertips to get the most from small group time. To avoid interruptions, design this space to include everything you and your students might need. Use what you have at your school to get started. Here are some basic materials you'll want as you set up a small group instructional space. (Also see suggested materials for each developmental reading stage in Sections 2–5.)

1. Little books for guided reading

2. Pencils to keep at the table

3. Wall space or bulletin board behind you

4. Sticky notes, index cards, markers, scissors, highlighter tape

5. Dry erase Focus Board

6. Dry erase markers and erasers

7. Guided reading lesson plan

8. A table and seating for students

Images:
1,2,4,6,7. Debbie Diller
3. iStock.com/Pongasn68
5. iStock.com/clubfoto
8. iStock.com/kampol Jongmeesuk

How Do I Set Up a Small Group Space?

Set up a small group teaching space where you can see every child in the classroom. This will help you monitor learning expectations for the rest of the class when you're working with a small group. Having a table for home base for small group will provide a dedicated learning space where kids can focus as they work together.

Small group area set up in a corner space before school starts. There is a wall and dry erase board behind the table for use during small group instruction. Portable shelving can be placed to the right for storage.

A table anchors this small group space in kindergarten. A cabinet and shelves nearby hold teaching supplies. Materials for individual children are well-organized: magnetic letters on cookie sheets and writing supplies in small white baskets.

Provide ample space for each student at the table. If possible, have a seat for each child so they don't have to drag chairs from their desks to the table. You might use placemats or adhesive-colored table spots to define spaces and help young learners focus.

You'll want shelves for small group storage in this area, too. Set up your small group table near built-in shelving if you have this option. Or place shelves behind your table to organize your books and other small group teaching materials.

It's handy to have blank wall space or a bulletin board or a dry erase board behind your small group space. That way you can post reminders for small group, such as your weekly schedule or anchor charts you might use for reference during small group lessons.

Try to keep your small group area organized. This will help you and your students focus during small group meetings.

ONLINE LEARNING TIP: Set up a small group area for online groups in a similar way as you would for face-to-face teaching. But add space for your device and a document camera.

ONLINE LEARNING TIP: Keep materials needed for online learners simple: device, paper, pencils, and the link to the text they will be reading. If you can, provide dry erase materials, too.

Rectangular table, angled in a corner, creates an inviting small group area. Shelves and a file cabinet hold teaching supplies. The teacher has a bird's-eye view of the whole classroom, including the adjacent Independent Reading station.

Large adhesive dots designate workspaces at this small group table for young readers. Matching stools are made from overturned plastic buckets. Portable shelving stores small group materials, and a dry erase board is available for displaying charts.

At-home learning space for online learners uses a trifold board and a place to sit at a table. A clock helps kids learn to tell time and follow a posted schedule.

What Do I Include *in a* Small Group Lesson?

Small group lesson formats will vary depending on the purpose of each small group. Think about your students and what you want them to gain from being in the group. As you plan and teach in small group ask:

- What do I want the child to learn as a reader, writer, thinker, or speaker in today's small group?

- What kind of support does each learner need to be successful?

- How will I determine how much support to provide to each student in the group?

- Do the materials we'll use match the purposes of this group?

- What instruction will I provide?

- What will the kids practice? What will they read, write, and speak about?

- What kind of small group will best accelerate these students?

Levels of Reading Development

Small group time is the heart of differentiation. It should not be one-size-fits-all. What you include in each lesson may differ slightly based on the needs of the group you are working with. Early readers have different needs than fluent readers!

So, instead of planning one small group lesson and just tweaking it slightly for each group, plan intentionally for the needs of your students. Use information from students' developmental reading stages to guide your planning and instruction. If you work with multilingual students, consider their level of language, too.

In each section of this book, you'll find ideas geared to specific developmental reading stages instead of grade levels. Use these to help you decide on a focus for each group. If you have students reading on an emergent level, regardless of grade level, go to Section 2. If you have students reading at the transitional stage, use Section 4 for small group lesson ideas.

You may notice that I do not use the term *nonreaders* in this book. Instead, I use *emergent* readers to name students who bring language and understanding to school even though they may not yet be decoding. You may have newcomers learning a new language in your classroom. These children may have more fluency in their native tongue. Immerse them in oral language and help them listen and speak before jumping into just phonics and decoding. Oral language is the foundation for all reading and writing children will do at school and beyond. Use what they know and build on their strengths.

Reading and Writing Components

It's important to include literacy components that match what kids need in each small group lesson. To help you make decisions, this book and the online companion contain charts with key reading behaviors for a variety of developmental stages. You will also find in Sections 2–5 specific teaching ideas for each of the following components matching its stage.

Here are some general considerations when planning and teaching:

- **Comprehension** (Emergent, Early, Transitional, and Fluent Stages)

  - Comprehension should be at the forefront of all small groups, whether kids are reading, writing, or speaking. We should help kids make meaning in every small group lesson.

  - If you work with emergent readers, the focus is on oral language and comprehension. Kids may be comprehending stories read to them, or they may be reading little books on their own.

  - Ask a variety of questions including higher-level ones, to be sure children are thinking about what they're reading, regardless of the stage of reading.

  - Comprehension demands increase across reading levels.

  - By the time kids are at the fluent reading stage, rich discussions should take place if kids are in guided reading groups, inquiry groups, or book clubs.

- **Phonics (and Phonological/Phonemic Awareness)** (Emergent, Early, and Transitional Stages)

  - Kids need a systematic approach to learning phonics. Phonological and phonemic awareness should precede phonics instruction.

  - Phonics emphasizes letter-sound relationships. It involves the associations between sounds and how they are represented in print.

  - Phonics understanding enables children to decode words quickly and easily, which leads to greater fluency and enables the brain to better comprehend.

- Be sure kids have phonological awareness before adding print (phonics). Children should be able to recognize and manipulate *sounds* within words they hear *before* they do this with letters.

- Phonemic awareness is the ability to manipulate the smallest speech sounds in the language. It is part of phonological awareness.

- Be sure you understand phonics elements before teaching them. See Some Helpful Phonics Terms in the online companion for clarity.

- **Fluency** (Emergent, Early, and Transitional Stages)

  - Fluency includes oral reading rate, prosody (or phrasing), and reading with intonation and expression.

  - Emergent readers are just learning to look at print and don't read fluently. They need fluency with letter sounds and high-frequency words to begin breaking the code. Emergent readers are learning to focus their eyes on each word as they point and read.

  - Begin to work with oral reading fluency with kids in the early reading stage to help them look more closely at print and move their eyes across a page.

  - Transitional readers often need the most work with fluency because they are reading longer, more complex texts.

  - Recognizing high-frequency words quickly impacts readers' fluency because it lightens their cognitive load. Help students develop rapid recognition of these words at the emergent and early reading stages.

- **Vocabulary** (Early, Transitional, and Fluent Stages)

  - It is important for children to have large oral vocabularies so they can understand the words they are reading.

  - Students' word knowledge combined with understanding a topic impacts comprehension.

  - Help students at all levels pay attention to new words while listening to texts read aloud and independently.

  - At the emergent and early reading stages, most vocabulary will be developed orally.

  - Children at transitional and fluent stages will learn many new words by reading.

  - Encourage students to use new vocabulary when speaking and writing.

- **Writing** (Emergent, Early, Transitional, and Fluent Stages)
  - Children's writing will look different from one stage to the next. Use the Early Developmental Writing Stages chart found in the online companion as a reference. Celebrate each stage to encourage more writing.

  - Focus on writing craft (e.g., ideas, voice, word choice) before moving into conventions such as punctuation and capitalization.

  - Help students use the books they are reading as models for writing, too.

  - Children's writing often mirrors the books they are reading. Emergent readers often write patterned sentences just like the books they can read. Early readers include more sentence variety as they write. Transitional readers write more complex sentences, and students at the fluent stage incorporate dialogue, figurative language, and technical vocabulary as they compose. Consult your state standards for specifics expected at your grade level.

- **Print Awareness** (Emergent Stage)
  - Print awareness is developed in the emergent reading stage.

  - Concepts about print include holding a book right side up, turning pages correctly, and knowing that reading moves from top to bottom and left to right with return sweep. Children learn to identify the front cover, back cover, and title page of a book.

  - Emergent readers should learn the difference between a letter and a word and recognize that sentences are composed of words separated by spaces.

  - Emergent readers learn to identify all uppercase and lowercase letters.

  - One-to-one tracking develops as emergent readers understand word boundaries.

Choosing an Instructional Focus

Instead of trying to include every literacy component in every small group lesson, choosing an instructional focus helps to accelerate children's learning. Putting less in a *lesson* allows kids to try one or two things that will help them become better readers, writers, or speakers by the end of a small group meeting.

A focus is a short-term goal. For example, an emergent reader may work on pointing to each word while reading (one-to-one matching). An early reader may focus on using chunks to decode short words. A transitional reader might have the goal of reading in phrases, while a fluent reader's goal may be to pay attention to figurative language.

Choose a focus that will bring kids the most benefit in these short bits of time. Don't just meet in small groups. Accelerate students by pinpointing specific reading or writing behaviors that will move them forward. Use the Key Reading Behaviors charts included in this book and in the online companion. (Each section in this book has specific ideas on how you can help students work with the focuses that match their reading level.)

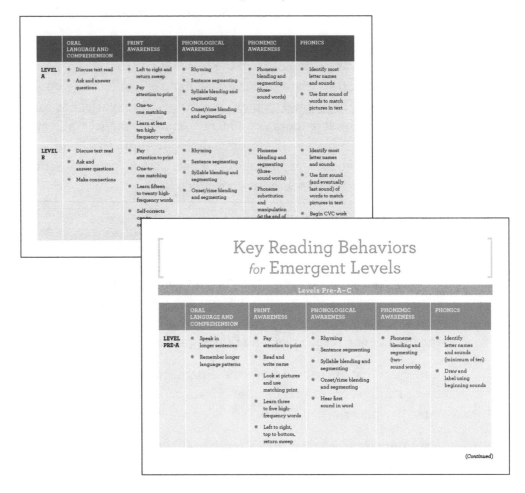

Stick with a focus for multiple lessons. Having a focus works better than asking kids to decode one day, comprehend the next, read for fluency on a third read, and then look for new vocabulary words at the end of the week. Practicing the same reading behavior on multiple days with a little support from you or their peers helps these become habits.

Change the focus when students are demonstrating the desired reading (or writing) behavior more independently. When you no longer need to assist them with a literacy behavior, move to a new focus. It may take three or four small group lessons; you might change the focus weekly. The change of focus depends on your students and the reading behavior. Observe your kids carefully, and they will show you what they need next.

Using a Focus Board

My favorite small group teaching tool—a Focus Board—is simple to make and use. Just grab a small dry erase board (9-x-12) and a plate stand to make a quick and easy stand-up Focus Board. Use skinny dry erase markers to write "FOCUS" at the top of the board. Then quickly jot down the reading (or writing) behavior kids will focus on using during the small group lesson.

When kids come to the small group table, start by having them read today's focus. Then provide a quick demo of this focus behavior to make sure kids know how to do it and why it's important. Use the Key Reading Behaviors charts to choose the focus.

If you work with emergent or early readers (or dual language learners), add a visual to help kids remember what you want them to try. See the online companion for sample Focus Boards with visuals for emergent and early readers (**resources.corwin.com/simplysmallgroups**).

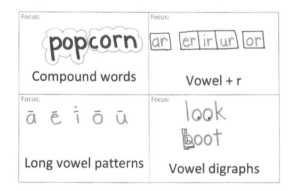

Sample Focus Boards used in small group.

Selecting Text

After you've formed a group and chosen a small group lesson focus, select the text. In the past, I'd look at a group's reading level and find a new book on that level. If kids were reading at Level G, I'd go to the book room and pick up a few new titles at that level for the group. But I found that many times I was teaching kids how to read *that book* instead of helping them become readers who could read not just this book but the next ones after that!

Instead of grabbing any Level G book, I now look at the reading behaviors kids might need at that early reading stage using the reading behaviors suggestions. If it's a group that needs to work with phonics patterns, such as *oo*, *ou*, or *ow*, I look for a Level G book that has words with those patterns in it. This way students will get focused practice with reading work that will stick.

Likewise, if I'm working with a group reading at Level G that needs to use punctuation for reading in phrases, I will look for a book that is written in phrases to give kids support for learning this reading behavior.

Consider genre, subject matter, and content when selecting text for small group. Seek out books and articles that match students' cultures and interests. Don't downplay reading motivation. But don't overwhelm yourself finding the perfect book. Get in there and give it a try. Planning gets easier as you get to know the books available to you.

These are some sample reading behaviors and the kinds of text you might look for at a variety of stages. Additional information is in matching sections throughout this book:

ONLINE LEARNING TIP: In small groups, encourage children to keep mics unmuted, if possible. This helps them learn to take turns having a conversation before and after reading.

READING STAGE	FOCUS READING BEHAVIOR	KIND OF TEXT TO USE
Emergent readers	Decode CVC words	Text with some CVC words to decode
Emergent readers	Use high-frequency words	Books with repetitive use of those high-frequency words
Early readers	Decode words with common long *a* vowel patterns (*ae*, *ai*, *ay*)	Text with one-syllable words that have long *a* vowel pattern
Early readers	Self-monitor and reread as needed	Books that are a bit more difficult and may require kids to reread
Transitional readers	Use genre characteristics to comprehend fables	Fables at matching reading levels
Transitional readers	Notice new vocabulary and stop to figure out what words mean	Text with some unfamiliar (or bold) vocabulary; books with glossaries
Fluent readers	Discuss character traits, changes, and relationships	Stories where strong relatable characters change and have conflicts

Before, During, and After Reading

Be sure kids are doing the work in small groups. It can be tempting to give them too much support so they'll be successful. In many teacher-led groups, children will be reading books at a level where they need just a bit of support. Plan carefully for what your role will be *before*, *during*, and *after* the reading in a small group lesson. Think about what the group members will be doing, too. Here's a quick overview to help you plan:

	STUDENTS DO	TEACHER DOES
Before reading	• Read the Focus Board and demonstrate understanding • May practice phonics skills needed for reading this text • Preview the text and make predictions, set the purpose for reading	• Models the focus reading behavior • May lead a brief phonics skill lesson related to today's book • Introduces the text
During reading	• Read the text as independently as possible • Try the focus reading behavior as they read • Interact with the text (e.g., using sticky notes) and think about what they're reading	• Listens in to readers and prompts, as needed • Has a conversation with individual readers
After reading	• Have a discussion with others about what they read • Show how they used the focus reading behavior today • Reflect on their learning in small group	• Asks higher-level questions to promote deeper thinking • Supports students as they show what they tried • Reminds kids to keep trying this

ONLINE LEARNING TIP: During reading in small group, put children in the waiting room to read. Then bring them back, one at a time, to listen to and confer with them about what they read.

This book includes a variety of small group options. All groups will not have a before, during, and after reading component. For example, emergent readers may meet for phonological awareness or letter work. Fluent readers may meet in a book club or writing group. Use ideas from each section in the book to guide your small group planning and teaching.

Family Involvement

ONLINE LEARNING TIP: After reading, have students use a virtual tool to mark something on a page related to the reading behavior they tried (e.g., circle words with long *a*, show your virtual sticky notes).

With the increasing use of technology and online learning options, we have an unprecedented opportunity to help family members support their children's learning at home! From the start of the year, establish a strong relationship with parents and caregivers to build trust and respect. Investing time in patiently and frequently answering questions and sharing information with parents goes a long way in helping children feel safe and learn at school or at home.

Caregivers' anxiety affects the emotional state of their children. Calming and reassuring parents sets a foundation for smooth transitions to our new ways of teaching.

Here are some tips for working with parents and caregivers, based on my experience as a teacher, parent, and caregiver:

- Recognize and celebrate different kinds of involvement and support, such as those shown in the examples below. Try not to judge but rather appreciate and celebrate them all.

  ○ A caregiver who cannot read but volunteers to cut out laminating

  ○ A parent who has little free time to support learning outside of school but donates resources to the class

  ○ A family member who reads and plays games with their children each night

- Give grace to families as they navigate technology but maintain high expectations.

- Use brief text messages to communicate with families whenever possible. It's quick and easy! You might get a Google phone number for school use or an app like Talking Points so caregivers don't have your direct number.

  ○ Call parents and caregivers individually. Invite them to tell you anything they might want you to know about them or their child.

- ○ Ask them about their hopes and dreams for their child.

- ○ Provide two or three positive things you have noticed about their child.

- These words can comfort caregivers who are unsure about new and changing forms of learning and teaching.

  - ○ I'm here to help.

  - ○ I understand.

  - ○ We can do this!

  - ○ Let's work together to help your child.

- Learn about each child's culture and home language. You might ask caregivers to teach you a few words in their home language if it's different from the language taught in at school.

- Encourage caregivers to use the same academic vocabulary (e.g., *character traits, comprehension, central idea, text features*) with their children as you use in small group instruction. You might periodically send home short lists of academic vocabulary children are learning to use, so families can practice with these same words at home. For reference, use the Teacher Talk sections from my Simply Stations books.

- Share the Key Reading Behaviors chart that matches the child's current reading level to help adults at home understand how to help their children grow as readers and writers. This information can help caregivers be realistic and reduce stress for everyone! Point out what families can do at home to help students work toward grade-level success.

- If a student is not reading at grade level, show a book the child *can* read alongside a text that reflects grade-level reading. Emphasize that children progress at different rates and celebrate success along the way, even if students aren't reading at grade level. Also, talk with families when a child might need additional support or services as part of your documentation.

- Don't tell parents and caregivers that a child is *reading* at a certain level if that child can't comprehend what was read. Instead, say that the child is *decoding* at that level and needs to work on comprehension to move forward.

- Send home familiar books for students to read, so they can experience success with at-home reading.

ONLINE LEARNING TIP: Schedule online conferences, as needed. Through these, we can reach more families than ever, especially if work schedules make it difficult for them to attend conferences at school.

2

Teaching Emergent Readers

Characteristics *of* Emergent Readers

Children at the *emergent reader* stage are sometimes also referred to as *pre-readers*. They are typically in preK or kindergarten and are just beginning to learn to look at and use print. But you may have students in other grades at this stage, too. Children just beginning to learn English as a new language may be emergent readers in English but more proficient in their home language.

At the beginning of this stage, children are developing oral language, may read or write their names, and may identify a few letters and sounds. They like to play with words and are learning to manipulate sounds in words as they rhyme, clap syllables, and hear words in sentences. They are learning about how print works and may scribble write, make mock letters, or use letters to write the first sounds of words.

By the end of this stage, emergent readers are paying attention to print. They have developed phonological awareness. They know most of their letters and sounds and use these to read and write consonant-vowel-consonant (CVC) words (e.g., bat, lid, sun) in isolation and connected text. They read and write simple stories and informational books. Corresponding guided reading levels are pre-A through C. There is a big range of skills here, so I've included specific ideas based on each reading level.

Emergent Readers and Comprehension

When working with emergent readers, begin with listening comprehension, especially in whole group. Have children listen to and talk about stories and informational text. **Listening comprehension** develops prior to reading comprehension. Students must understand stories and information read to them *before* they can understand similar texts they read on their own.

Read aloud stories and informational text geared to young readers. Read books multiple times to enhance learning opportunities for children as they listen and speak about characters or new information learned. Think aloud, making your reading process visible to students: *I wonder what the character is going to do next. Look at her face. I think she is going to . . . What do you think?* Or, *This book is about different kinds of rocks. I can tell by looking at the photo of rocks on the cover. The title is* Rocks. *It starts with rrrr.*

ONLINE LEARNING TIP: Record yourself reading stories and information children will want to revisit. Post these along with whole group lessons online for kids to view multiple times. Archive for future reference.

Invite children to chime in with you on repeated parts of stories, fill in rhyming words at the ends of sentences and nursery rhymes, and tell their connections and questions. This rich oral language experience will enhance comprehension over time.

Give emergent readers opportunities to "read" the books you've read aloud on their own. Students will do exactly what they've seen modeled. Have them talk about the pictures and say parts of the story they remember. You'll probably notice them pointing to the words and sounding just like you—even if they can't yet read the words. This oral language is the beginning of emergent reading comprehension.

EL TIP: Have multilingual children look at the pictures in a book and talk about them before reading to build vocabulary. Let them listen to stories read aloud and talk, draw, and write about them, too.

ONLINE LEARNING TIP: Practice sharing text before teaching to ensure that emergent readers can see the books or modeled sentence writing correctly. Be sure children are not viewing a backward image. Join your online meeting using another device (e.g., phone, Chromebook) to be sure everything looks right.

Start *by* Looking *at* What Students *Can* Do

It's important to meet with emergent readers in small groups to help them learn how language and print work. The charts that follow can guide you in planning small group instruction based on what you see children are able to do. Use these strengths to help kids accelerate to the next level. For example, emergent readers can talk about pictures in books. Prompt them to *speak* in sentences that expand in length to develop their oral language. Help them use new vocabulary as they speak.

Children don't need to know *every* letter and *every* sound to start learning to read. Teach a few consonants and short vowels to begin. Knowing the letters and some matching sounds in a child's name is a good starting point. Kids also need listening and oral language to be able to read. They need to *hear* and *play* with sounds before they can map those sounds onto letters that make words. They need to be able to talk so they will understand the words that are written in print.

Acknowledge emergent writing as students at this stage use mock letters and drawings. Ask children to stretch out words and say each sound as they write it. Have them use an alphabet strip with pictures for support as they learn more about letters and sounds. Have children read their writing. Jot what they say on a sticky note to remember the message communicated.

The chart that follows shows what emergent readers may be able to do across the levels from pre-A to C.

EL TIP: Use pictures of things they can name easily to help multilingual children learn letters and sounds. Also be sure they can easily form the letters you are working with in writing to give them confidence.

ONLINE LEARNING TIP: Create a brief video for parents and caregivers on how (and why) to assist their child but not give the child the answers during online learning.

Emergent Readers May Be Able to . . .

LEVEL PRE-A	LEVELS A AND B	LEVEL C
• Listen to the text and talk about it	• Listen to stories and talk about characters, setting, and plot	• Listen to stories and informational text and retell/respond
• Speak in sentences (five to six words/sentence)	• Listen to informational text and tell what they learned	• Use pictures and matching words to read text with less predictable patterns
• Have well-developed vocabulary	• Speak in more complex sentences with details	• Continue to pretend read more complex stories and text by talking about the pictures
• Talk about pictures	• Use pictures and matching words to read simple text with predictable patterns	
• Pretend read and point to words	• Pretend read increasingly complex familiar stories and point to words	• Name most letters and say their sounds
• Sing ABC song	• Name many letters and say their sounds	• Read and write beginning and ending sounds of words
• Know the first letter of their name		
• Recognize environmental print	• Read and write their first name and recognize names of classmates	• Know twenty or more high-frequency words
• Handle books	• Know five to twenty high-frequency words	• Reread to self-correct
• Know some letters and/or sounds	• Pay closer attention to print	• Write letters to represent the beginning, middle, and end sounds in words
• Write mock letters, letter strings, or a letter representing the first sound of a word to label a drawing or make a list	• Write a letter representing the first sound, then the last sound, and eventually the middle sound in a word	

Plan *and* Teach Lessons That Match *the* Development Level *of* Your Students

As you work with children at emergent reading levels, start with text they can read easily with just a bit of support. This will motivate them to keep trying! Help them to write simple messages, too, as they are learning about print.

There are many things young children must think about as they read: What is this book about? What sound does that letter make? How do I blend those sounds together? Do I already know that word? What's in the picture? Does this make sense? And as writers they must be able to segment sentences into words and words into sounds as well as think about which letter makes which sound . . . and how to form those letters. Whew!

At emergent levels, teach students to point under each word to help them pay attention to print. Teach high-frequency words that match the books they will read. These words are used as anchors—words they know. Help children apply letter–sound knowledge and use pictures as support for comprehension.

Be mindful as you work with emergent readers. You are helping them establish foundational skills. Spend time helping them develop phonological awareness—hearing sounds before moving into phonics. Don't rush your students. Get to know them and this important reading stage so that you can help your students build strong knowledge and skills.

MATERIALS NEEDED for SMALL GROUPS at the EMERGENT STAGE

- Sentence strips, blank white paper
- Pencils or black markers
- Pointers (e.g., chopsticks, drink stirrers)
- Name puzzles
- Alphabet arc
- Magnetic letters and cookie sheet
- Familiar objects or pictures

(Continued)

- Favorite rhyming books from read-aloud

- Nursery rhyme songs, charts, books, and raps (see the online companion for familiar nursery rhyme printables)

- Word Wall (or Sound Wall) with words on cards with magnets on back (interactive)

- Picture cards with familiar objects that represent one-syllable words (e.g., cup, rug, pen, lamp, dish)

- Environmental print

- Big books from shared reading with high-frequency words being learned (Levels pre-A and A)

- Leveled books with one to two lines of print and predictable sentence patterns and high-frequency words (Levels A and B)

- Leveled books with two to three lines of print and CVC words and high-frequency words (Level C)

- Decodable readers with CVC words (when students are paying attention to print)

- Elkonin boxes

- Puppet with a movable mouth (for phonological and phonemic awareness)

- Whiteboards and dry erase markers

- Letter/sound chart for students to refer to

MATERIALS NEEDED for ONLINE SMALL GROUPS

- Paper and markers

- Virtual Word Walls (use a Google Slide with a 5-x-5 table inserted)

- Virtual alphabet arc: https://www.esc4.net/rla/interactives

- Short nursery rhyme rap videos

- Nursery rhyme readers: https://www.readinga-z.com/books/poetry-books

- Digital leveled readers

- Rhyming games with sound: https://www.education.com/game/match-rhyming-words

- Virtual Elkonin boxes and counters: https://toytheater.com/elkonin-boxes

- Drive-through family pickup of materials, including whiteboards and dry erase supplies, name puzzles, picture cards, and leveled and decodable books

What *to* Look *for in* Emergent Reader Text

Texts change quite a bit from Levels pre-A through C, and there are variations among books even within a level. You may be tempted to print out pages with dots beneath each word to help students with one-to-one matching. Instead, look for little books with a few words children know and that match their needs and interests. Give them real books with colored pictures and photos that look like them. Help them feel like real readers!

- Books and texts at **Level pre-A** usually have one high-frequency word that is used on each page with a matching picture. The patterned sentences have only one to three words. Or, there may be an alphabet letter with one word to match each page of an ABC-related book.

- **Level A** books have about eight pages of highly patterned text with strong picture support. If students can read the first page, they can usually read the rest of the book. These texts can help children begin to learn about print and how it works.

- At **Level B** the pattern usually changes a bit, but there is still high picture support. Many of the same words will be repeated in the book but not in the same order on every page. More high-frequency words are used, and students must be able to apply sound knowledge to letters they see, especially the first letter. You might use simple decodables at this level, especially those with two-letter words (e.g., *at, up, in, go, no, me*), but be sure these books make sense!

- By **Level C** children are paying very close attention to print! They should know at least twenty to twenty-five high-frequency words and be able to decode CVC words as they read. Well-written decodable readers with CVC patterns can be helpful at this level. Using short books with word families is beneficial, too. Picture support is still strong at this level.

ONLINE LEARNING TIP: Make sure all your supplies are prepared before the lesson begins. Send communication to students and families about what to have ready for a small group lesson before it begins.

Consider the following when looking for text for readers at Levels pre-A through C:

- Will your children connect to this book? Is it about something they know or are interested in? Do the people in the book reflect their cultural heritage in a positive way?

- Does this book make sense? (Some decodables really don't!)

- Do the pictures support the meaning of this text?

- Does this book match what your students need to practice (e.g., only a few words on a page for one-to-one matching, high-frequency words, CVC words)?

- Are you giving kids both fiction and nonfiction texts to read?

- Are you exposing children to a variety of texts from a variety of publishers (each company's books will have their own look and feel)?

- Are your students reading books (or just sheets of paper)?

- Are you giving your children opportunities to read print as well as digital versions of text?

Books at level A (top), level B (middle), and level C (bottom) show how text changes at the emergent reader stage.

Let's dig into what a small group might look like at each of the emergent reader phases. The examples that follow provide a selection of formats for planning what to teach in small group, depending on level and student needs. Printable lesson planning templates for emergent readers are found in the online companion at **resources.corwin.com/simplysmallgroups**.

I've included suggested numbers of minutes for various parts of the lessons. These are simply guidelines; use what you know about your students to adjust times accordingly.

Lesson Plan Format
for Emergent Readers

Meet with your children at Level pre-A in small group for ten to fifteen minutes, depending on the attention span of your learners. You might think about the Level pre-A lesson as a "pick two" format. There are four areas of focus work to choose from: **oral language** and **print awareness, phonological and/or phonemic awareness, phonics**, and **writing**. Try to include a bit of phonological awareness in every lesson. (Later in this section, starting on page 58, you'll find Focus Work sections that detail each of these areas.)

Pick two focus areas per lesson that will impact your students' literacy. Look at the chart Key Reading Behaviors for Emergent Readers to help you choose reading behaviors to focus on in small group lessons. You can find a printable version online at **resources.corwin.com/simplysmallgroups**.

For example, you might have children look at the pictures and retell a familiar book, like *The Three Bears* (**oral language**). Then work with a few letters (**print awareness**), ending with having students find several words containing those letters. You might show the book cover and have kids point to the letter that says /b/.

Or, have children orally make up a sentence about the book and clap the words to segment the sentence (**phonological awareness**). Then do interactive writing (**writing**) of that sentence. Your goal is for students to be successful, so keep things simple!

It helps to have a Focus Board with visuals posted during each lesson. You'll find some printable Focus Boards in the online companion.

Follow your children's lead as you teach in small groups. You might teach the same lesson several days in a row or vary lessons as students need something different. The sample lesson format on the next page provides considerations for working with children at Level pre-A.

Sample Lesson Format: Level Pre-A

WHEN WORKING WITH STUDENTS AT LEVEL PRE-A, PICK TWO TO FOCUS ON WITH YOUR SMALL GROUP:	
Oral language focus work	<ul><li>Have students speak in sentences with expanding complexity (more words and higher-level vocabulary)</li><li>Include a book or a picture of something kids know</li><li>Do shared reading of a Level pre-A book or retelling of a familiar read-aloud book</li></ul>
Print awareness focus work	<ul><li>Start with children's names, using name puzzles or games</li><li>Do letter work, using tactile materials (e.g., magnetic letters)</li><li>Kids read, build, mix and fix, and write a high-frequency word from the Level A list; have them find it in a book, too</li></ul>
Phonological awareness, phonemic awareness focus work	<ul><li>Work with phonological awareness (larger units of speech) before moving into phonemic awareness (smallest speech sounds)</li><li>Use picture cards or say words (emphasis is on working with *sounds*, not print)</li></ul>
Writing focus work	<ul><li>Do interactive writing where you share the pen with the group to write a sentence; children write the parts they know</li><li>Cut up the sentence, word by word, and have children rearrange these into a sentence as they point and read under each word</li></ul>

Small Group Reading Lesson Plan
for Emergent Readers, Level Pre-A

Group: blue

Date: November 5

Book Title: *No, David!*

Level: familiar read-aloud

Oral Language Focus	talk about pictures retell a familiar book (expand sentences orally) Pass *No, David!* around the group. Have each student tell something about the story, using the book and pictures for support. Help children speak in expanded sentences. Ask questions to help children include more words: *What else happened? How did the characters feel? Say it again and tell more.*
Print Awareness Focus	children's names letters (high-frequency words) shared reading Ask students to point to words they know (e.g., *no*).
Phonological or Phonemic Awareness Focus	rhyming sentence segmenting blending and segmenting syllables (onset-rime) phonemes Play Onset-Rime Thyme. Say a one-syllable word (classmate's name or familiar object), starting with the onset (sound before the rime) and then the rime (vowel and letters after it). Have children blend the sounds to say the word. (*P-aul, Sh-ane, L-ou, b-ook, c-up*). For segmenting, give kids the word and have them say the parts.
Writing Focus	interactive writing cut-up sentence

My Notes:

This book worked well. Kids love it and could find the word *no.* I helped them think about the sounds in the word *no.* Continue to work with blending and segmenting onsets and rimes.

Lesson Plan Format
for Emergent Readers

at Levels A and B

If your students are reading at Levels A and/or B, meet with them for about fifteen minutes. Use the sample lesson plan template to jot down your plans using leveled guided reading or decodable books.

Use a Focus Board with visuals during each lesson, too. See samples below. Follow your children's lead as you teach in small groups. You might stick with the same focus for several days in a row and use multiple books.

(You'll find printable lesson plan templates and Focus Boards with visuals in the online companion, **resources.corwin.com/simplysmallgroups**.)

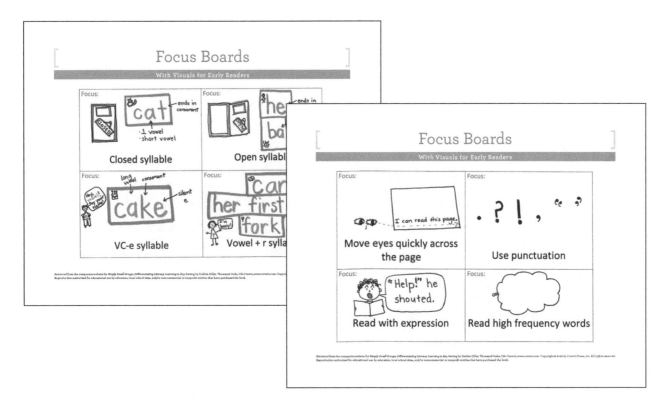

Start your lesson with phonological or phonemic awareness work, as needed. Choose ideas from the focus work sections later in this section, which start on page 58.

Here's a sample lesson for Levels A and B to get you started:

Sample Lesson Format: Levels A and B

WHEN WORKING WITH STUDENTS AT LEVELS A AND B, INCLUDE THE FOLLOWING:	
Phonological or phonemic awareness or phonics focus (one to two minutes)	• Look at the continuum of phonological and phonemic awareness, and work with children where they are. Be sure they can hear bigger units of sound before moving into phonemes (smallest sounds). • Continue to expand letter–sound knowledge, especially in the context of reading and writing sounds they know. • Work with blending two-sound words.
High-frequency word work (one to two minutes)	• Practice with high-frequency words children need for the book they are currently reading to help these words "stick." • Have kids build and find words in the text.
Reading behavior to focus on (one minute)	• Use a reading Focus Board with visuals. Show students what you expect them to do as readers today.
Before reading (three to five minutes)	• Have students talk about the pictures and predict what the book will be about. • Build a few high-frequency words needed to read this book. • Set the purpose for reading. Read to find out . . .
During reading (four to five minutes)	• Be sure to listen to individuals and prompt while the others read on their own. • Have students read on their own in a quiet voice. Try not to have this be choral reading by staggering who starts. • Have children read the book several times on their own.
After reading (three to four minutes)	• Discuss what the kids read. • Ask a higher-level question. • Have students take turns finding the high-frequency words and reading a sentence with that word in it.

Some teachers do a follow-up lesson and have children write using the same instructional focus the next time they meet with a group. Use ideas for a writing focus, which can be found starting on page 84. See the lesson plans that follow for samples. Blank templates are available online at **resources.corwin.com/ simplysmallgroups**.

Small Group Reading Lesson Plan
for Emergent Readers, Levels A–C

Group: green	**Date:** October 10
Book Title: *I Can See*	**Level:** A

Warm-Up

Key Reading Behavior Focus Work

Phonological Awareness, Phonemic Awareness, or Phonics:

Beginning sounds: What do you hear at the beginning of *teacher*, *nurse*, *pilot*, *plumber*, *can*, and *see*?

Have students say the sound and then write the first letter on a dry erase board.

High-Frequency Word Work:

Play "Our Pile, My Pile" with the words *I, can, see, a, the*

*remind about today's focus

> **Focus Board Idea**
>
> Focus: **the**
>
> Point under each word

Before Reading

Book Introduction

This book is about people I can see. Read to find out who the people are.

Find the word *I*. Point under each word as you read it.

Find the word *can*. Point under the word. Read *can* as you point to it. How do you know the word is *can*?

During Reading

My Notes

After Reading

Discussion Questions

1. Who was in the book? What people did you see?
2. How are the people the same?
3. Compare a teacher to a _____.

Follow-Up Lesson

Reread Text and Write

What we will write:

A sentence that might be in this book. *I can see _____.*

Say the sentence and have kids count the words.

How we will write:

Interactive writing (share the pen) and cut-up sentence.

Group: Ruth and Oscar

Date: December 2

Book Title: *How Many Legs*

Level: B

Warm-Up	**Key Reading Behavior Focus Work** Phonological Awareness, Phonemic Awareness, or Phonics: 1. Clap syllables. Ask, *Will it be a long or short word?* (animals, legs, elephant, frog, spider) 2. What sound do you hear at the beginning of *legs*? What letter will you see in the beginning of *legs*? What do you hear at the end of *legs*? What letter will it be? Find *legs* in the book. Repeat for *how*. High-Frequency Word Work: Play "The Match Game" using *these, have, many, how, do, to, we.* Help kids pay attention to letters and sounds. *remind about today's focus	**Focus Board Idea** Focus: Blend sounds (onset and rime; phonemes)

Before Reading	**Book Introduction** This book is about animals and how many legs they have. Read to find out how many legs the animals in this book have.
During Reading	**My Notes**
After Reading	**Discussion Questions** 1. How many legs did the animals have? 2. What's another animal that could be on page 5? Why? 3. Which page would you be on? Why?
Follow-Up Lesson	**Reread Text and Write** What we will write: A chart with a title showing animals and the number of legs each has. How Many Legs Do the Animals Have? | cat	4
-------	-----
dog	4 | How we will write: Interactive writing, share the pen

Lesson Plan Format
for Emergent Readers

If your students are reading at Level C, meet with them for about twenty minutes. Use the blank sample lesson plan in the online companion to jot down your plans using leveled guided reading or decodable books.

Use a Focus Board with visuals in each lesson. Follow your children's lead as you teach in small groups. You might stick with the same focus for several days in a row and use multiple books.

(You'll find printable lesson plan templates and Focus Boards with visuals in the online companion, **resources.corwin.com/simplysmallgroups**.)

Include phonological or phonemic awareness work, as needed, before moving into the phonics portion of the lesson. Choose ideas from that focus work section that begins on page 72.

Have kids read the new book as independently as possible. As you listen to individuals read during a small group, prompt children to use the phonics patterns being studied. Try not to fix every decoding error kids make. Get students to do as much of the word as they can. Your role should be to help children use what they already know how to do as readers. If you notice students pausing or getting stuck, try one of the following:

- What do you see that can help you?

- Put your finger under that word. What do you know?

- You stopped. Is it making sense?

- Use your finger. Say each sound as you point. Blend the sounds. What's the word?

- When you come to this in another book, you'll know what to say.

Here's a sample lesson format for Level C groups to get you started.

Sample Lesson Format: Level C

	WHEN WORKING WITH STUDENTS AT LEVEL C, INCLUDE THE FOLLOWING:
Phonological or phonemic awareness or phonics focus (two minutes)	• Do phonics work with several CVC words. (Do phonemic awareness with three-sound words first.) • Use Elkonin boxes to help students apply letter–sound knowledge. • Begin to work with word families at the end of Level C to expand students' word knowledge.
High-frequency word work (two minutes)	• Practice with high-frequency words children need for the book they are currently reading to help these words "stick." • Build a few new high-frequency words needed to read this book.
Reading behavior to focus on (two minutes)	• Use a reading Focus Board with visuals. Show students what you expect them to do as readers today.
Before reading (four to five minutes)	• Help kids read the title and talk about the cover to predict. • Let them skim the book to get an idea of what it's about. • If there is new vocabulary (beyond CVC words), talk about the new word using pictures in the book. • Set the purpose for reading. Read to find out . . .
During reading (four to five minutes)	• Listen to individuals and prompt while the others read on their own. • Have students read on their own in a quiet voice. This is *not* choral or round robin reading. • Have children read the book several times on their own to develop fluency.
After reading (four to five minutes)	• Discuss what kids read. • Ask a higher-level question or two. • Have students take turns sharing new words (especially CVC words) they read in the text.
In the next lesson . . .	• Reread the book (three to four minutes). • Review high-frequency word work (two minutes) and phonics/phonemic awareness work with CVC words (two minutes). • Have students write in response to what they read (ten to twelve minutes).

It's important for students to write following the reading of a book. But it's too much to do this in one sitting! Take the time to have kids reread the book and then write in small group. See ideas for writing focus work on pages 84–91. Sample lesson plans follow. Again, a blank template is available online at **resources.corwin.com/simplysmallgroups**.

Small Group Reading Lesson Plan for Emergent Readers, Levels A–C

Group: A.J, C.D., M.P., A.T. **Date:** December 2

Book Title: *At the Fair* **Level:** C

Warm-Up	**Key Reading Behavior Focus Work** **Phonological Awareness, Phonemic Awareness, or Phonics:** Use Elkonin boxes to push and then write sounds (big, cup, long, fast) High-Frequency Word Work: Play "How Many in a Minute?" using *you, the, can, little, what, at, your* Help kids pay attention to letters and sounds. *remind about today's focus Focus Board Idea — Focus: — *sat* — Blend the sounds (CVC words)
Before Reading	**Book Introduction** Read the title. Have you been to a fair? What can you ride there? Read to find out what you can ride at the fair in this book.
During Reading	**My Notes**
After Reading	**Discussion Questions** 1. What can you ride at the fair in this book? 2. What was the biggest ride? What was little? 3. What would you ride? Why?
Follow-Up Lesson	**Reread Text and Write** What we will write: A connection (e.g., *I can ride the cups that spin.*). Talk first about going to a fair and what rides kids have been on or would like to go on. How we will write: Students write a sentence on their own. Help them use sounds they can hear as they write.

WHEN READING WITH CHILDREN
in ONLINE SMALL GROUPS

1. Have students unmute themselves if possible.

2. Before reading, teach them how to take turns talking about the book.

3. During reading, place all but one student in the waiting room to read on their own. Listen to that child read and confer for a minute or so.

4. Then place that student in a waiting room while you bring another child into your meeting space to confer. Try to meet with as many students as you can. Keep it brief.

5. After reading, encourage kids to take turns talking about the book. Then have them show how they used the instructional focus from today's small group lesson.

The remainder of this section contains specific suggestions for instructional focus work related to key reading behaviors for emergent readers. You'll find information and photos of work that will engage young learners and accelerate their developing skills. Here's how to use this information simply to plan and teach in small groups. Find the matching focus work to meet the needs of your students:

1. Start with **oral language and print awareness focus work**, including high-frequency words, for students who are just learning to look at print, especially at Levels pre-A or A. Begin with what they know—speaking. Then move into print work. You'll find ideas below for oral language, working with letters and sounds, high-frequency words, and nursery rhymes to name a few.

2. **Phonological and phonemic awareness focus work** is critical throughout the emergent stage. Use the suggestions on pages 84–87 to help students from Levels pre-A through C develop understanding of *spoken* words, syllables, rhymes, and individual speech sounds. Include this work in every lesson so it is well-established by the end of the emergent stage.

3. Move into **phonics focus work** (see pages 81–83) as students demonstrate phonological awareness. Children must be able to hear and manipulate sounds before mapping them onto print. By the end of Level C, children should be able to read and write many three-sound words.

4. I've included **writing focus work** as a separate piece, but it is related to all three of the above. Some children will learn as much or more about print from writing as they will from reading, so include writing often.

Choose Matching Oral Language *and* Print Awareness Focus Work

Oral language is a foundation for all reading and writing students will do over the years. Build a strong base by spending time in small group to help emergent readers develop listening and speaking skills. **Print awareness** is the understanding that print carries meaning, that letters make words that can be written and read. It includes learning how to hold a book and turn the pages, reading from top to bottom and left to right. Children with high print awareness recognize and write their names and begin to point to words they know (e.g., *I, a, no, like, can*) in books as they read.

Consider these things as you choose oral language and print awareness work for small groups:

- Talking about familiar objects and books is time well spent for children with low or limited oral language, especially at Level pre-A.

- Children reading at emergent levels should talk about the pictures in their books to develop oral language and support comprehension, too.

- Children at Levels pre-A through B are just learning about print. Their names are usually the first words they learn to read and write, so use names to develop print awareness at Level pre-A.

- Take time to help students pay attention to print through Level B. They will be learning high-frequency words to use as anchors as they track print by putting their finger under each word. Learning to write some of these same words will give them confidence as writers.

- Print awareness is usually firmly established once children are reading at Level C, so it will no longer be an instructional focus.

- By the end of the emergent stage, children understand what a word is and typically read and write quite a few high-frequency words. They will use letters and sounds to decode and write simple three-sound words.

In small group, continue to help students use oral language to make meaning of the texts they read. The books emergent readers *can* read are simple. The text typically has a limited number of words and controlled vocabulary. But children can still comprehend and think about the meaning of the words and pictures.

Plan a variety of questions and include one or two that promote higher-level thinking about what kids read. Encourage children to speak in sentences as they talk about what they read and write. Include **comprehension** in every lesson so children understand that reading is more than just decoding.

QUESTIONS to DEVELOP HIGHER-LEVEL THINKING at the EMERGENT LEVEL

- *How do you think the characters in this book feel? How can you tell?*

- *What else might the characters do? Why do you think this?*

- *What might happen if . . . ?*

- *What would be different in this story if the setting (or characters) changed?*

- *Let's think of another page we could include at the end of this book.*

- *Let's compare _____ to _____.*

- *Show us another way . . .*

Choose from the following as you plan oral language work in small group lessons for your emergent readers.

Oral Language Focus Work

It's important to have students always speak in sentences. Encourage them to expand their language by saying, "Tell me more." Have them retell stories heard and read, speak in longer sentences, and talk about things they know. Help them ask questions of each other to increase language and vary sentence structure. This builds a foundation for later reading and writing.

LEVEL PRE-A ORAL LANGUAGE FOCUS TEACHING TIPS

- Support children to speak in longer sentences. Record how many words they usually use in a spoken sentence. Your goal is to have students add another word or two to a sentence by the end of a lesson. Ask questions to help children include more words: *What else happened? How did you feel? Say it again and tell more.*

- Have children talk about familiar books and situations. This will build their confidence and skill. Have them retell stories by using the pictures.

- Use pictures about things kids know as a catalyst for their talk, too.

LEVELS A–C ORAL LANGUAGE FOCUS TEACHING TIPS

- Have children look at the cover and pictures in a book before reading and talk about what they notice.

- Look at specific pictures and use new words kids will need, especially in nonfiction books. Have children use that vocabulary orally before they read (e.g., Teacher says: *A helicopter can go. Have you ever seen a helicopter? What do you know about helicopters?* The student might say: *I saw a helicopter on a roof. Helicopters are in the sky. Helicopters are really loud.*)

- Teach children to think before reading and tell what they think will happen or what they will learn. As they read, have students check and confirm or change their predictions.

- Have a brief conversation with each child as you listen to them read a bit on their own. Ask them about what they have understood in a book so far.

- After reading, be sure to talk about the book. Ask a variety of questions, including at least one higher-level thinking question.

Following are photos of some small group oral language ideas. Find the focus in bold that matches what your students need. Grab some books, a few pictures, and a hand puppet, and let's get started!

Each child talks about a page or two to **retell a familiar story** as you pass the book from child to child. Encourage students to use vocabulary from the book by prompting them with that word.

EL TIP: Use familiar books representing the cultures of your children in small group. Invite kids to say native words in their language.

ONLINE LEARNING TIP: Show a familiar picture book using a document camera. Or use a PDF version. Ask students to take turns talking about pictures as you show the pages.

iStock.com/zenstock

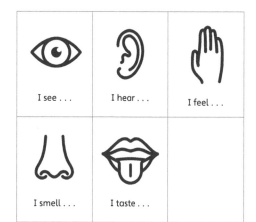

Image source: iStock.com/Happy_vector

| I see . . . | I hear . . . | I feel . . . |
| I smell . . . | I taste . . . | |

Have students do **sensory talk** about an interesting object or photo. They take turns telling a sentence about the item using their senses. Use cards with pictures representing each sense to prompt their talk. Sensory talk cards are available in the online companion.

ONLINE LEARNING TIP: When doing oral language activities with children online, have them take turns speaking. Include every student and be sure kids are doing more of the talking than you.

EL TIP: Record students' talk and play it back. Listening to themselves can motivate multilingual learners to speak!

Play **Repeat the Sentence**. Hold a parrot puppet to your ear and pretend it is talking to you. Then tell the children a sentence and have them take turns repeating it. Start with three- or four-word sentences. Increase sentence length as children remember longer sentence patterns.

ONLINE LEARNING TIP: When having kids answer chorally online, ask children to mute their mics. This will minimize audio feedback. Read their lips as they speak. It will get easier as you practice this technique.

Print Awareness Focus Work

Children need **print awareness** to read and write. This important work is typically done at Levels pre-A through B, starting with reading and writing their **names** at Level pre-A. Names are the first thing babies and toddlers usually learn to say. Likewise, their names and the names of other important individuals (e.g., *Mom, Dad, Pap, Nana*) are the first words children typically learn to read and write. At Level pre-A, kids start to notice environmental print (e.g., *McDonald's, milk, Doritos, stop*). They may even say, "That's like my name!" Students may ask how to write a few words they want to use as they learn that talk can be written down.

Help children at Level pre-A develop an interest in **letters**. Present alphabet activities in playful, tactile ways, connecting to the ABC song and letters in their names. Always include letter experiences using manipulatives so kids can learn about special features of sticks, circles, dots, and curved lines in letters. Have children practice forming letters using big muscle movements from top to bottom and left to right.

Print awareness includes helping emergent readers learn a few words they will recognize quickly and easily. At Levels A through C, teach **high-frequency words**, which are words used most frequently in print. (These become sight words as we learn to read them quickly and easily.) High-frequency words help to anchor children's reading, especially when a known high-frequency word starts a sentence. As students read and point under words, using high-frequency words as anchors, they develop one-to-one print matching at Levels A and B.

Here are some considerations when helping emergent readers develop print awareness:

- When playing letter or word games, be sure some of the letters or words are known. Move from known to new to build confidence and skill.

- Use tactile materials to develop letter and word knowledge. Have children identify letters and sounds with magnetic letters, manipulate word cards, and use dry erase materials to create neural pathways to the brain.

- Always help children read *and* write letters and words from top to bottom and left to right.

- Teach high-frequency words that children will need in the books they are reading. See ideas on pages 67–71.

- As children read, remind them to point *under* each word so they can see them. (Kids at Levels pre-A and A sometimes put their finger *over* the word.)

LEVEL PRE-A PRINT AWARENESS FOCUS TEACHING TIPS

- Teach children to read and write their first name with a capital letter. Have them write standing beside a large dry erase board to write using large muscles first.

- Use an alphabet arc to help children organize letters and understand their relationship to each other.

- Have kids trace or write using sandpaper letters, sand, shaving cream, hair gel packets, or big paintbrushes and water outdoors.

- Ask students to point to a letter, word, picture, period, and so on. When they point to words and pretend to read familiar read-aloud books, they are showing an understanding that print carries a message.

LEVELS A AND B PRINT AWARENESS FOCUS TEACHING TIPS

- Continue working with letters and sounds. Play games with magnetic letters and alphabet arcs.

- Teach and encourage children to find high-frequency words in books and in the world around them.

- You might give children little pointers (e.g., witch's fingers) to point under each word as they read. Help them monitor to be sure they have enough words or aren't making up too many words. They should develop one-to-one correspondence.

- Help students write sounds they hear as they write.

LEVEL C PRINT AWARENESS FOCUS TEACHING TIPS

- Students should now have high print awareness.

- They may still point under each word to monitor their reading.

- Continue high-frequency word work at this level. There are many words children need to know how to read and write quickly and easily at this level.

Following are photos of fun ways to help emergent readers develop print awareness in small groups.

Students play with **name puzzles** made with a laminated white envelope with their typed name, as shown. Include matching letters inside and a dry erase pen. Students build their names and say the name of each letter, working from left to right. Then they mix up the letters and repeat. Finally, they write (or trace) their name on the envelope with a dry-erase pen.

Make a **name-matching** game using photos of your students and their names printed on cards in black ink. Have them match the names, read the names, write the names, or say sentences using names. Play "find the name" by giving clues (e.g., *that starts with /s/, that rhymes with _____, that ends with /m/*). Do name sorts (e.g., boys and girls, long or short hair, number of letters in the name).

Make simple books with **environmental print**. Have children bring in labels they can read. Glue one per page and have students point and read these books. Have them find a picture that starts with a sound, ends with a sound, rhymes with a sound, and so on.

An alphabet arc is a graphic organizer for **letter learning**. Kids name and place magnetic (or plastic) letters on it in order as they sing the ABC song for support. Start with A and work to Z. Taking turns with a partner, one child places and names A, the next B, etc. When done, they remove and name each letter (in order from A to Z) for practice. Do this same work with letter sounds, too. Name a sound and have kids pull down that letter.

EL TIP: When teaching letter sounds, show students letters that match sounds they already know in their home language (e.g., /b/, /f/, and /m/ all make the same sounds in Spanish and English).

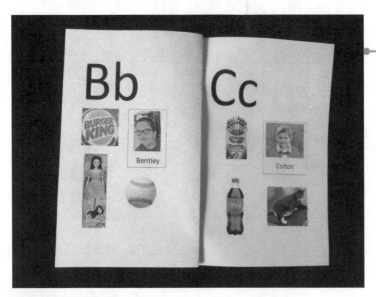

Make simple **ABC books** with students. Use student names, environmental print, and pictures of favorite things or people. Include the upper- and lowercase letter, a photo, and a word label on each page.

ONLINE LEARNING TIP: Send home magnetic letters for emergent readers if possible.

Children do a **letter–sound match**. Place pictures of known objects on the table. Hand out magnetic letters that match the first (or last or middle) sounds of the pictures. Have kids take turns saying the sound and name of their letter and place it on the picture it matches. Mix and repeat. Later, add word cards to match the pictures. This time students name the picture, say the sound of their letter, and place it on the matching picture and word cards.

High-Frequency Word Focus Work

Learning high-frequency words is an important part of print awareness. Knowing a few words quickly and easily helps children develop fluency and confidence as readers and writers. Choose words to teach with intention. I've provided a sampling of high-frequency words for emergent readers found in books they will be reading on page 262 and in the online companion.

Often lists of high-frequency words are sent home at the beginning of the school year for parents to practice with children. Some kids learn these words quickly and easily, but others do not. I recommend limiting the number of words sent home to five at a time. After kids have mastered those, send home the next list. You'll find printable lists to send home in the online companion at **resources.corwin.com/simplysmallgroups**. Adapt these to meet the needs of your children.

Here are some considerations when working with high-frequency words at the emergent reading stage:

- Some high-frequency words are easy to decode, but others (e.g., *said, of, to, is, you, the, to, from*) must be learned by heart. Remind kids to use the sounds they know, such as /s/ and /d/ in *said*; /t/ in *to*; and /fr/ and /m/ in *from*.

- Give children practice with the high-frequency words you are teaching in connected text, not just in isolation. Use very short poems (four to six lines), predictable patterned text, or nursery rhymes for shared reading with these words. (I've included nursery rhyme printables in the online companion to use in small groups.)

- Reading high-frequency words over and over in a variety of places will help emergent readers learn them more quickly and easily.

- Have emergent readers do multisensory work with high-frequency words. Let them build the words with magnetic letters, mix up the letters, and rebuild the words, saying each sound from left to right.

- Have students write high-frequency words with dry-erase materials, running their fingers under the word and rereading it.

- Work with high-frequency words that will be in the little books students will read in small group as part of the lesson warmup.

LEVEL PRE-A HIGH-FREQUENCY WORD FOCUS
TEACHING TIPS

- Teach children that *A* and *I* are letters and words. Have them find these in books and on the walls and identify them as letters or words. Expose children to a few other high utility words, such as *can, go, to, the,* and *like*.

- Do shared reading of predictable text on charts or books at Level A that include these words.

- Make predictable books or charts with print students know (*I go to ___. We like to play with ___.*) Include student names and photos.

LEVELS A AND B HIGH-FREQUENCY WORD FOCUS
TEACHING TIPS

- Have children look closely at high-frequency words and use the sounds they know to read them quickly.

- Work with high-frequency words that have only two sounds to blend (e.g., *up, at, an, it, am, on, in*). When kids know a few short vowel sounds and some consonant sounds, these two-sound words will be easier for them to remember.

LEVEL C HIGH-FREQUENCY WORD FOCUS
TEACHING TIPS

- As you teach CVC (or CCVC or CVCC) words, it will be easy for children to learn high-frequency words with that pattern (e.g., *has, yes, that, this, went, when, with*).

- Many high-frequency words can be decoded easily and work well as flashcards.

- Always look at the books kids will be reading in small group to be sure there are opportunities for them to practice reading the high-frequency words you are teaching.

- Encourage children to use these high-frequency words as they write, too.

Choose from the following as you plan high-frequency work in small group lessons for your emergent readers. Use the photos for inspiration. You'll find the focus in bold.

Have children find **high-frequency words** in a familiar short text. Have them name the letters in the word, move their body to match (tall letters: reach to the sky, short letters: squat down). Give them magnetic letters to build the word from left to right. Place or find the word on the Word Wall.

TIPS for HIGH-FREQUENCY WORD WORK ONLINE

Use Google Slides to make a slide show with high-frequency words kids are learning.

- Limit yourself to about three to five different words but use duplicates of the words so kids get additional practice.

- Play the slideshow to have them practice the words.

- You might add a voice recording of each word.

- One possible resource, https://online-voice-recorder.com/, is free and easy to use. Kids just click on a button to hear the word and self-check.

EL TIP: Most high-frequency words don't have much meaning in isolation, so help English learners use these words orally in sentences to help them develop language as well as print awareness.

Play **Our Pile, My Pile** with high-frequency words written on index cards. Use words children know well with a few new ones added. You might use children's names at Levels pre-A and A. Place cards facedown and turn them over one at a time. Words kids read quickly go on "our pile." If only one child says it fast, the word goes on "my pile." The goal is to make "our pile" the largest.

Play **Guess the Word**. Show a list of high-frequency words your students have been learning. Or use your Word Wall. Choose one of the words and ask kids to number a dry erase board from 1 to 4. Use the pictured clues, and have children write one of the words on their boards to guess the words. It's okay if they get it correct the first time. They will write it four more times! Have them write and then read each word as they guess.

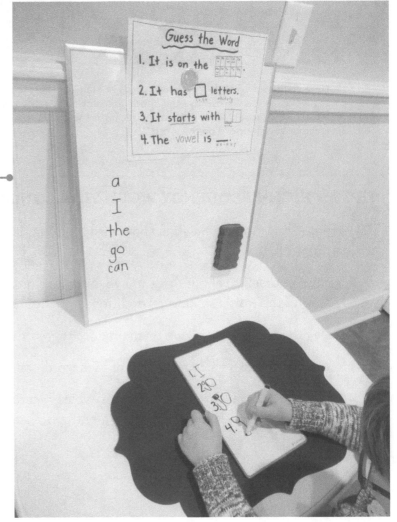

Do **shared reading of predictable patterned text**. Review high-frequency words in the text. Give each child a pointer. Have them point to and name the high-frequency words in the text. Use a predictable text (Level A book or chart). Children point to each word and "read" it together.

EL TIP: Predictable text has lots of repetition, which can help multilingual learners learn oral language patterns and read high-frequency words.

Display a **nursery rhyme** containing several high-frequency words being studied. (Use printables from the online companion.) Do shared reading of the nursery rhyme. Then have kids take turns pointing to and reading high-frequency words in the rhyme. Or have them match high-frequency word cards to the rhyme, naming each word.

Choose Matching Phonological Awareness

and Phonemic Awareness Focus Work

Foundational skills, such as phonological awareness, phonemic awareness, and phonics, are necessary for students to learn to read. **Phonics**, which emphasizes sounds and how they are represented by print helps with decoding, and once kids can figure out words with ease, they can read and write more fluently, which opens space for deeper comprehension. (Find specific suggestions for phonics focus work in the next section, beginning on page 81.)

But be sure children have phonemic awareness (or can *hear* sounds in words) before adding print and working with phonics. Students at the emergent stage need phonological awareness and phonemic awareness *prior* to learning phonics.

Remember that **phonological awareness** includes an understanding of *spoken* words, syllables, rhymes, and individual sounds. **Phonemic awareness** is the understanding of *individual* speech sounds. (**Phonemes** are the smallest speech sounds in spoken language.) Learning to hear and manipulate the smallest sounds, or phonemes, lays the foundation for phonics, reading, and writing. Start by playing with sounds and using pictures or objects.

The charts that follow will help you plan for foundational skills work that will accelerate or propel emergent readers forward. While these charts provide the *what* and *why*, you'll find the *how* in the Focus Work sections, starting on page 75.

Keep these things in mind when choosing foundational skills work:

- At Level pre-A, choose to focus on one or two of the following skills each time you meet with your small group. Your goal is to develop children's language, including listening and speaking. Focus on helping kids hear sounds and speak in ever-expanding sentences.

- At Levels A and B, include phonological awareness and phonemic awareness skill work at the start of a lesson. Choose work that matches the needs of your students.

- By Level C, most students should have developed phonological awareness. Focus on phoneme blending and segmenting prior to having students work with related phonics.

EL TIP: When working with children learning English as a new language, be explicit when showing them how to make new sounds:

- Have them look at your lips and try it.
- Give them small hand mirrors to watch their own mouths as they make new sounds.
- If masks are required in your classroom, wear a face shield during small group so children can see your mouth.

FOUNDATIONAL SKILLS FOR LEVEL PRE-A	WHY?	WORD STUDY ELEMENT
Rhyming (*cat, hat, mat, that*)	This will help students with word families in phonics, over time.	Phonological awareness
Sentence segmenting (*The cat climbs up a tree.*)	Helps kids understand what a word is as they clap or count words in an oral sentence.	Phonological awareness
Syllable blending and segmenting (*ta-ble, but-ter-fly*)	Hearing syllables will eventually help students decode as they look at syllable rules in phonics.	Phonological awareness
Onset-rime blending and segmenting (*c-up, l-ake, s-ock*)	Eventually kids will decode using chunks (*c-at*). Hearing these first will help them when print is added.	Phonological awareness
Phoneme segmenting and blending (*n-ō, m-ē, p-ī*)	Move to individual speech sounds once kids can blend onset-rimes. (Start with two-sound words.)	Phonemic awareness
Letters and sounds	Children need to learn at least ten letters and sounds to progress as readers.	Phonics

FOUNDATIONAL SKILLS FOR LEVELS A AND B	WHY?	WORD STUDY ELEMENT
Rhyming (cat, hat, mat, that)	This will help students with word families in phonics, over time.	Phonological awareness
Sentence segmenting (The cat climbs up a tree.)	Helps kids understand what a word is as they clap or count words in an oral sentence.	Phonological awareness
Onset-rime blending and segmenting (c-up, l-ake, s-ock)	Eventually kids will decode using chunks (c-at). Hearing these first will help them when print is added.	Phonological awareness
Phoneme segmenting and blending (c-a-t, sh-i-p, ph-ō-n)	This is needed before students can decode CVC words. (Move to three-sound words.)	Phonemic awareness
Letters and sounds	Children need to learn at least ten letters and sounds to progress as readers.	Phonics
Decoding CVC words (at the end of Level B)	As students approach the end of Level B, they have developed high print awareness and may start to decode CVC words in text.	Phonics

ONLINE LEARNING TIP: Work with your grade-level team to create prerecorded lessons for whole group that match the needs of emergent readers. Take turns making these and share with your team to reduce everyone's workload. But don't prerecord small group lessons. You need to be there with kids to guide and support them.

FOUNDATIONAL SKILLS FOR LEVEL C	WHY?	WORD STUDY ELEMENT
Rhyming (*cat, hat, mat, that*)	This will help students with word families in phonics, over time.	Phonological awareness
Phoneme segmenting and blending (*c-a-t, sh-i-p, ph-ō-n*)	This is needed before students can decode CVC words. (Work with three- and four-sound words.)	Phonemic awareness
Phoneme substitution and manipulation	This will help kids understand that changing out letters makes new words.	Phonemic awareness
Decoding CVC words	As students approach the end of Level C, they have developed high print awareness and may start to decode CVC words in text.	Phonics

It can be difficult for children to hear and produce sounds when wearing masks, dealing with tech issues, or both. Here are a few options:

- Wear a transparent mask just while teaching phonological awareness or phonics

- Wear a face shield behind a plexiglass screen while teaching sounds in reading

- Prerecord short lessons for phonological or phonemic awareness with pauses for kids to respond (so they can see your mouth) and use these in small group

Phonological Awareness Focus Work

Phonological awareness includes rhyming, sentence segmenting, and blending and segmenting of syllables, then onsets and rimes, and finally phonemes, the smallest units of sound. Always ensure that children have phonological awareness before moving into phonics.

Phonological awareness work gives kids opportunities to play with the sounds of language *without print*. Use these activities multiple times in any order that meets the needs and interests of your students.

Keep these things in mind when choosing phonological awareness work:

- Rhyming will help kids read and understand word families at the end of the emergent reading stage.

- Sentence segmenting will help writers know that words create sentences.

- Manipulating parts of words lays a foundation for decoding words, including multisyllable ones at later reading stages.

EL TIP: Multilingual children can echo read, dramatize, and memorize nursery rhymes, and they can listen for rhyming and other sounds. Nursery rhymes help kids develop vocabulary, pronounce new words, and boost confidence.

Here are photos of some small group phonological work ideas. Gather a few simple materials—nursery rhymes, plastic counters and cups, along with Elkonin boxes—and have fun playing with the sounds of language! Find the focus in bold that matches what you'll be teaching.

Kids listen for rhyming words (exaggerate them) as you read or recite a **nursery rhyme** together. Ask, "Do these words rhyme?" Give two words from the rhyme. Students say *yes* or *no*. Or they give thumbs up or thumbs down to answer. Have students *tell* rhyming words from the nursery rhyme (e.g., *Jill, hill*; *down, crown*).

Play **Count the Words**. Give each child five to seven counters and a cup. As you say a sentence, they drop a counter into the cup each time they hear a word. (e.g., in *Miguel has a new sister*, they use five counters). Then they repeat the sentence in unison, removing a counter from the cup for each word spoken. Have them count the words. Work on expanding sentence length over time.

EL TIP: Sentence segmenting can help kids understand sentence structure as they learn a new language. Start with short sentences (three or four words long).

ONLINE LEARNING TIP: Use Count the Words in combination with Sensory Talk from oral language lessons. This works well virtually or in person.

EL TIP: Include every child's name, even if the sounds are different from the language you are teaching. Point out similarities and differences between the sounds in both languages.

Do **syllable blending and segmenting**. Say a word (e.g., child's name or familiar object), one syllable at a time, with a clap for each syllable. Have kids blend the syllables to say the word. (Start with two-syllable words.) Use this for calling kids to the table, dismissing them, or asking them to find an object. For example, *Joc-e-lyn, Mar-cus, pen-cil, cray-on*. For segmenting, give kids a word and have them say and clap it syllable by syllable.

Use only one-syllable words for **Onset-Rime Time**. Say a one-syllable word (classmate's name or familiar object), starting with the onset (sound before the rime) and then the rime (vowel and letters after it). Have children blend the sounds to say the word. For example, *P-aul, Sh-ane, L-ou, b-ook, c-up*). For segmenting, give kids the word and have them say the parts. As a variation, give kids the rime and have them add an onset to say the word and complete the action: *-y* (fly, as pictured), *-alk* (walk, talk), *-op* (hop, chop), *-augh* (laugh), *-un* (run), *-ile* (smile), *-ap* (clap, snap, flap), *-aint* (paint), *-ead* (read), *-ing* (sing).

Phonemic Awareness Focus Work

Phonemic awareness is under the big umbrella of phonological awareness. Phonemes are the smallest units of speech sounds. For example, in the word *sheep*, there are five letters but three phonemes—sh, ē, and p.

It's important for children to be able to manipulate speech sounds so they can later map letters onto those sounds and decode. Work with *sounds* only when doing phonemic awareness. After kids can hear sounds in words, then add letters and move into phonics.

NOTE: When doing phonemic awareness work, be sure to only use **one-syllable words**.

Children **segment and blend sounds** using their bodies or Elkonin boxes and counters. They listen to a two-sound word and move their hand from their shoulder to their wrist, as pictured, saying each sound.

Or they push a counter in each Elkonin box from left to right as they say each sound. (Use the printable in the online companion at **resources.corwin.com/simplysmallgroups** or a virtual one if doing distance learning.) Then they pull each counter down, segmenting the word into individual sounds before blending the sounds and saying the word again (e.g., *be, day, see, to, we*).

ONLINE LEARNING TIP: Virtual Elkonin boxes can be found at https://toytheater .com/elkonin-boxes. You can adjust the number of boxes from two through five.

Children listen and **blend phonemes** to guess a word. Slowly say the sounds in order, starting with two-sound and then three-sound words. When students can do this well, have them segment the words, one phoneme at a time.

To **manipulate phonemes**, children listen to a CVC word (e.g., *sun*) and repeat it. Then they say the first, middle, or end sound. Next, they build the word with magnetic letters and Elkonin boxes. After that they will change the first, middle, or end sound and point to that box. Finally, they take away a letter (e.g., /s/) and put a different sound there (e.g., /r/). Kids use magnetic letters to do this and say the new word (*run*). Repeat with other CVC words.

EL TIP: Be sure multilingual learners can make the speech sounds you're asking them to manipulate. Start with sounds that are the same in their home language and the language of instruction.

Choose Matching Phonics Focus Work

All children need systematic phonics to learn to read. There should be a planned, sequential set of phonics elements that are taught explicitly and methodically. **Phonics** knowledge allows children to decode words quickly and easily, thus freeing up their brains to comprehend.

Some considerations when choosing phonics work include the following:

- Students who have strong oral language combined with the ability to decode will have an easier time learning to read.

- Be sure to introduce phonics work thoughtfully. Work with phonics elements that match the stage where children are currently reading. For example, at Level B, students are decoding two-sound words. At Level C, work with three-sound words.

- Be sure students have strong phonological and phonemic awareness before moving into phonics work.

- Always include comprehension so children know that it's important to understand what they read.

While listening to individuals read during small group, prompt them to use the phonics patterns being studied. Try not to correct every error they make. Let them monitor and realize when something isn't making sense. If you notice children needing assistance, try saying one of the following dependent on the situation:

- You stopped. Is it making sense?

- You know those sounds. Blend them together. Does that make sense in this sentence?

- That's a word you know. Think about it. Use the sounds.

Use the phonics-focused activities shown in the following photos. The focus is in **bold**.

Kids use Elkonin boxes and dry erase markers to write **CVC words**. Show a picture of a familiar CVC object. Children name the object, then push and say each sound in order. Next, they write the letter to represent each sound in order, using an alphabet strip for support as needed.

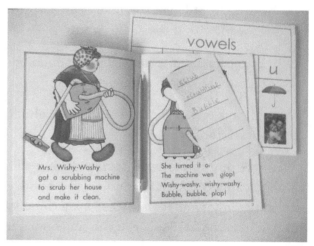

Make an anchor for one **short vowel sound** at a time. Start with *a*, then *o*, before moving to *e*, *i*, and finally *u*. Children read a list of CVC words and identify the short vowel sounds. They also use familiar books to go on word hunts for words with the short vowel sound they are studying. Have them make a list, then read each word and tell the short vowel sound in it.

☆

EL TIP: Multilingual students often have difficulty with short vowels. Work with short vowel sounds and word families a lot at Level C before moving to the next reading level.

Kids work with CVC words using the thirty-eight most common phonograms. Have them take turns placing different magnetic letters representing consonants in front of the chunk on a card. Each time they read the word as they explore a **word family** (e.g., -at becomes cat, sat, bat, rat, that).

ONLINE LEARNING TIP: Have online learners write the sounds on a piece of paper or a whiteboard and hold it up to the screen. Make anchor charts and post them online for student reference.

Choose Matching Writing Focus Work

Some teachers have kids read a book for a day or two, followed by a writing lesson around the same text. This can help children apply what they're learning about letters and sounds and high-frequency words as they write. For example, if students are learning consonant sounds, compose a message together and help that group write the letters representing the sounds they hear. You be the scribe and quickly fill in the other letters to write each word. Include writing focus work at the bottom of the lesson plan templates from the online companion, **resources.corwin .com/simplysmallgroups.**

First, decide on **what the group will write**, choosing from a variety of options:

- A sentence telling what the book was mostly about (e.g., *The dog ran away from home.*)

- A list of items from the book (e.g., *Toys: train, car, blocks, game*)

- Another page that could go in this book (e.g., *At the store we got some apples.*)

- A connection (e.g., *We like to play with toys.*)

- Something a character in the story would say (e.g., *"The horse is here."*)

Also decide **how you will write**. Here are a few suggestions:

- Interactive writing (share the pen and write together with each student contributing a word or part of a word to the message)

- Cut-up sentences (students put a sentence they've written back together, word by word)

- Students write a sentence on their own

- Each child draws a picture and adds a label

- Every child adds a word to a list

ONLINE LEARNING TIP: You might use a shared Google Doc or interactive whiteboard for online writing.

Don't worry if your students can't yet spell all the words as they write. This is a perfect opportunity to use phonological and phonemic awareness (e.g., count the words in a sentence you plan to write, segment the sounds in a word) and pinpoint appropriate phonics needs! Pay attention to what kids are using but confusing.

For example, if students write *j* for */ch/* in the word, *chair,* help them pronounce the */ch/* sound. Have them put their fingers in front of their mouths when saying */ch/* and */j/* and look in a small mirror. Your mouth is similar, but more air is released with the */ch/* sound. (Don't expect children at these levels to spell the *air* chunk. That comes in the early reading stage.)

Help children stretch out words and listen to the sounds in order. Have them count the sounds and think about which letters represent the sounds. They might use the book as a reference to check their spelling, too. If you are working on a phonics pattern, such as CVC, review that pattern and remind kids to think about its spelling as they write their words.

If children write on their own, spend a few minutes having them share their writing with the group. Teach kids to give compliments to each other first. Then ask them to look at the spellings related to the phonics patterns you're working on. You might have them use a colored pencil to circle that pattern in the writing they did. Remind them to keep thinking about that pattern as they read and write throughout the day.

EL TIP: Help children learning a new language write sounds they know. Point out how this sound is the same or different from the sound representing that letter in their native language.

EL TIP: Have multilingual learners talk in response to what they read before writing. Do lots of work around oral language before moving into writing.

Here are a few photos showing writing techniques to use with emergent readers.

Do **interactive writing** of a sentence the group creates about the last book they read. Say the sentence and have kids clap and count words (sentence segmenting). Children take turns using a marker to write sounds they hear in a word, adding to the sentence. The teacher writes the letters kids don't hear. Each time a new word is added, students reread the group's sentence and point to each word.

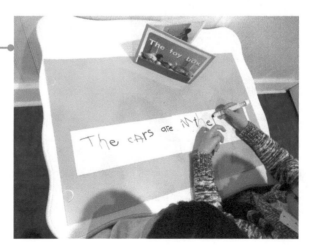

ONLINE LEARNING TIP: Use the interactive whiteboard option if available in your platform when teaching virtually.

Groups at Levels pre-A through B work with a **cut-up sentence**. Children point to each word as they read the sentence their group wrote interactively in the previous lesson. As the teacher cuts apart the sentence, word by word, children read that word. Then they work together to reassemble the sentence, pointing and reading each word to check. Mix up the words and repeat. To clean up, kids hand the teacher a word card as it's read.

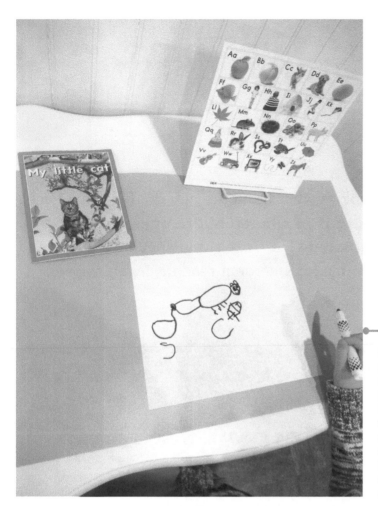

ONLINE LEARNING TIP: To do a cut-up sentence virtually, use flippity.net. Have students take turns helping to type each word on a sticky note and have kids put them in order to make the sentence. Or, use a Google Slide. Students help to type each word in a box. Then mix up the boxes and have kids take turns putting each box in order as they read the words together.

Have each child **draw and label** a picture in response to the book read in a previous lesson. They say the word, sound by sound, and represent each sound with a letter. Use this to assess students' letter–sound understanding.

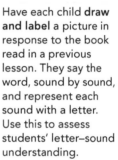

Children at Level C **write a response** on their own using an alphabet strip and short vowel anchor charts for support.

If You See This, Try This . . .

It's important to look at what students *can* do. But sometimes there are clear patterns of where children get stuck along a developmental continuum. Here are some specific solutions to common sticking points for emergent readers, level by level.

Level Pre-A

IF YOU SEE THIS . . .	TRY THIS:
Little (or no) letter knowledge	<ul><li>Start with the letters in their name only.</li><li>Make an ABC book with them. Use a picture of someone or something they know for each letter. Make tactile letters from sandpaper.</li><li>Work with the alphabet arc. Have kids point and sing the ABC song as they touch each letter.</li><li>Use magnetic letters, not letter cards, so they can feel the parts of each letter.</li></ul>
Low oral language	<ul><li>Ask the student to show a favorite person or object from home. Have them talk about familiar things.</li><li>Teach the child to record. Listening to oneself can produce more speech.</li><li>Provide part of the sentence for the child to repeat. Ask questions to produce more speech.</li></ul>
Needs name recognition or help writing name	<ul><li>Take a photo of the child. Add a name puzzle to match.</li><li>Provide a horizontal surface (dry erase wall) for the child to write on).</li><li>Let them trace their names. (Use large print and no handwriting lines.)</li></ul>

IF YOU SEE THIS...	TRY THIS:
Difficulty with rhyming	• Use familiar favorite rhyming books. Pause and have the child give the word (that rhymes). • Learn nursery rhymes and songs with rhymes. • Play matching games with rhyming picture cards (no print).
Trouble with phonemic awareness	• Start with two-phoneme words. Model how to blend. Blending is easier than segmenting. • When successful with two-phoneme words, move to words with three phonemes. • Adding objects or pictures that match the words can help at first.

Levels A and B

IF YOU SEE THIS...	TRY THIS:
Memorize language patterns in predictable text but don't pay attention to print	• Continue to work with high-frequency words and letter sounds. • Choose text with the same high-frequency words from page to page but with a pattern change (e.g., *We can go to the park. Can we go to the store?*). • Remind students to point to and look at each word as they read. • Be sure kids point *under* each word and don't cover the word with their fingers as they read.
Say more words than are on the page (make up text)	• Remind students to point to each word as they read. • If they say a word that's not on the page, ask them to point to *that word*. • Tell kids, "Point and match." • Use the cut-up sentence activity (see page 86).
Won't try to write letters but may draw	• Encourage children to write their names. (This is writing.) • Do interactive writing and share the pen to write a message about something they know (see page 85).

(Continued)

(Continued)

IF YOU SEE THIS . . .	TRY THIS:
Don't have one-to-one matching	• Choose text with known high-frequency words as an anchor. Have kids point to those words *before* reading. Remind them that their pointer should be *under* that word when they read the word. • Use the Make a Sentence/Cut-Up Sentence activity (see page 86). • Do shared reading in whole group. Have students hold the pointer.
Trouble with phonemic awareness	• Use three-phoneme words (if they can do this easily with two-sound words). Model how to blend. Blending is easier than segmenting. • Move to segmenting once they can demonstrate blending. • Adding objects or pictures that match the words can help at first.

Level C

IF YOU SEE THIS . . .	TRY THIS:
Skip words when they don't know them	• Say, "You read . . ." (and say exactly what the child read). Ask, "Is that what the book said? Which word did you skip?" Then help the child use known sounds and meaning (including the picture if it helps) to try the word. • Have the child reread the sentence with the new word.
Take a guess using some of the sounds in a new word	• Ask, "Did that make sense? Which word didn't make sense?" • Say, "You are making up words using some of the sounds. Stop doing that. Try the sounds you know *in order* to say a word that makes sense." • Help the child, as needed, and have the child reread the sentence with the new word.

IF YOU SEE THIS...	TRY THIS:
Get stuck on words they don't know and ask for help	• Have the child try something before just giving them the word. Ask them what they know. Have them use known sounds and meaning to try to figure out the new word. • Help the child and ask them to reread the sentence with the new word.
Slowly sound out every word in the text	• Tell the student, "You know the sounds. Blend them together to say the word fast, just like you were talking." • If the child is sounding out a known high-frequency word, say, "You know that word. Say it fast like you're talking."

EL TIP: If students are using sounds from their native language instead of the language you are teaching, tell them gently. Say, "In (your language) ___ says ___. In (the language we are learning) ___ says ___."

Teaching Early Readers

Characteristics *of* Early Readers

Children at the *early reader* stage are sometimes referred to as *novice* or *alphabetic readers*. They are typically in first grade but may be in other grade levels. These children are beginning to understand how words work. They can change sounds in words to make new words. (For example, they can change one letter to make *cat* become *sat* or *mat*. They can add *e* to *mat* to make *mate*.) Early readers can use phonics to decode many new words. They can read words using parts rather than just sounding out words one letter at a time.

By the end of this stage, early readers can decode most one- and two-syllable words using their knowledge of short and long vowel patterns and are learning syllable types. They've become flexible with letter sounds and know to try the other sound of a letter if the first one didn't work. Early readers work with more complex phonics patterns, including the sounds of /ou/, /ow/, /oo/, /ough/, and /or/. They are learning to decode silent letters like *kn*, *wr*, and *gn*.

Corresponding guided reading levels are Levels D through I. There are subtle changes from one level to the next that often depend on phonics knowledge. However, children at these levels also need to *comprehend*! Be careful not to focus so much on phonics that kids think reading is just decoding words. Always have them think about *what* they are reading and use *meaning* to help them solve new words, too. Include comprehension in every small group!

Early Readers and Comprehension

The goal of reading is to make meaning. In whole group, early readers are still developing *listening comprehension*, which is an important precursor to reading comprehension. Read aloud picture books and chapter books to your class, think aloud to model comprehension strategies, and have children talk about characters, setting, and plot in fiction.

Students benefit from hearing stories with more advanced vocabulary than they can read independently. Likewise, early readers can discuss central ideas and important facts in informational text read to them. Model how to use text features to locate information, too. Use your state standards to guide your instruction.

EL TIP: Students who are learning a new language and learning to read may need a longer time at the early reader stage because they are learning so many new sounds.

ONLINE LEARNING TIP: When reading aloud virtually, use texts in PDF or ebook format instead of holding up pages in front of a camera for kids to see. You can screenshare, which allows kids to see the entire page as you're reading.

EL TIP: Listening is a critical component of learning a new language. Be sure multilingual learners have plenty of time to listen and speak with peers about what they heard. Let them draw and write, too.

ONLINE LEARNING TIP: Send links ahead of time to online texts kids will read so they will have their "books" open and ready to read during small group time.

Fluency also affects children's comprehension. As kids read words quickly and easily, their brains are free to think about meaning. Many of the words they read are now *sight words*—words they can read rapidly because they have seen them many times. Continue to help students at this stage develop a large bank of high-frequency words. (Suggested words can be found in the online companion.)

Text for early readers has a wide range of punctuation and dialogue. Teach children at this stage to pay attention to punctuation and read fluently in phrases and with expression. This, too, will lead to improved comprehension.

EL TIP: Explicitly teach multilingual students punctuation marks in English and their home language. Help them see the similarities and differences in punctuation as they read, especially related to dialogue, questions, and exclamations.

Start *by* Looking *at* What Students *Can* Do

It's important to meet with students in small groups to build their skills and confidence. But it's even more important to plan for accelerating their skills to move them forward as readers and writers. Always have students at the early reader stage speak in sentences when working in small groups. Prompt them to tell more. This will develop their oral language, which will improve comprehension and vocabulary over time.

EL TIP: Provide sentence stems to help multilingual students speak in sentences in small groups. Use the same ones in whole group, too, for continuity.

ONLINE LEARNING TIP: When working with small groups online, be sure every student participates in the discussions. You may have to call on quiet students who don't normally volunteer.

Include writing in small group lessons to strengthen reading–writing connections. Help early readers move from being sound-by-sound spellers to writers who notice and apply phonics patterns being studied by the end of this stage. Use word hunts where children reread familiar text and find words with phonics patterns (e.g., long vowels). When they write, have them clap syllables. Also say, "Think about how that word looks in books."

ONLINE LEARNING TIP: Be sure online learners have pencil and paper or dry erase supplies handy during small group lessons. They can hold their writing up to the camera for the group to read together.

The chart that follows shows what early readers may be able to do, across the continuum from Levels D through I. It can guide you in planning small group instruction based on what you see children are able to do. Use these strengths to help kids accelerate to the next level!

Early Readers May Be Able to . . .

LEVELS D AND E	LEVELS F AND G	LEVELS H AND I
• Use oral language with vocabulary related to stories and information they are reading	• Make predictions and check on them	• Read longer books over several days
• Retell what they read	• Speak in expanding, more complex sentences as they retell	• Retell key events in stories using transition words
• Use pictures to support meaning	• Develop deeper understanding of story elements	• Develop deeper understanding of plot in longer stories
• Easily decode CVC words	• Notice text features in informational text	• Identify and use text features in informational text
• Blend and segment onsets and rimes	• Be more aware of long and short vowel sounds	• Decode one-syllable words with a variety of vowel patterns
• Know an increasing number of high-frequency words	• Know even more high-frequency words	• Use syllables to decode longer words
• Reread to fix up words	• Reread to fix up words and keep meaning going	• Use short and long vowel sounds flexibly
• Read without finger pointing to each word	• Read without finger pointing to each word; use fingers when stopping to figure out a new word	• Read more and more words by sight
• Write longer sentences	• Write most sounds they hear in words	• Reread sections while self-monitoring
• Use letters to represent sounds they hear, including vowels	• Try to use vowel patterns (but may not use the correct spelling)	• Start to read silently
		• Write most sounds they hear in words
		• Try to use vowel patterns (but may not use the correct spelling)

Plan *and* Teach Lessons That Match *the* Development Level *of* Your Students

As you work with children at the early levels of reading, the biggest change you will see from one level to the next is the range of phonics needed. Level D texts are shorter, have more picture support, and have more one-syllable words with short vowels or simple long vowel patterns. By Levels H and I, the books lengthen, are further removed from children's background experiences (especially the informational texts), and require decoding of more complex vowel patterns in multisyllable words.

Pay attention to children's decoding skills, but be sure to have students think about meaning, too, so that comprehension stays strong. You might do a bit of phonics work in isolation, but always move that decoding into connected text so children learn to apply those skills. In addition, expose early readers to fun, engaging text that will make them want to *be readers*.

MATERIALS NEEDED for SMALL GROUPS at this STAGE

- Dry erase supplies
- Laminated Elkonin boxes
- Cards with pictures representing one-syllable words (for phonics work)
- Word wall with high-frequency words on cards with magnets on back (interactive)
- Fiction books and informational texts at Levels D through I
- Decodable readers (with phonics patterns being studied)
- Anchor charts for vowel sounds
- Anchor charts with syllable patterns being studied
- Simple graphic organizers for comprehension
- Sticky notes and pencils
- Small whiteboard and plate stand for a Focus Board

MATERIALS NEEDED for ONLINE SMALL GROUPS

- Paper and markers (for writing)

- Virtual Word Walls (use a Google Slide with a 5-x-5 table inserted)

- Digital leveled readers

- Interactive whiteboard or a Google Slide for Elkonin boxes

- Drive-through family pickup of materials, including whiteboards and dry erase supplies, leveled and decodable books, simple graphic organizers, and sticky notes

What *to* Look *for in* Early Reader Text

Choosing the right text for early readers is essential! You want your students to experience success *and* the joy of reading. It may be tempting to print passages with controlled vocabulary, but ask yourself if these will promote a *desire* to read. Be sure to read the text before planning and teaching a lesson!

Keep these points in mind when choosing texts for early readers:

- The books early readers are learning to read in small groups contain many one- and two-syllable words in their oral language. But by the end of this developmental stage, children will be expanding their language with new vocabulary encountered in text.

- Books at Level D start with shorter sentences and fewer words per page and increase in complexity and length by Level I.

- Decodable texts have many words following phonics patterns kids are studying. But it is still important for children to use meaning to comprehend the texts they are reading.

- Informational text for early readers has a heavier vocabulary load than in the list type books students may have read at the emergent levels. Connect books to science and social studies topics being studied when possible.

- Understanding new words will influence children's comprehension, so it's important for them to pay attention to new vocabulary, too. Select text with a few new words but not so many that they interfere with comprehension. Talk with children about the meaning of some new words before they read, using pictures or video for support. Help students pause to figure out what new words mean, even if they can decode them.

ONLINE LEARNING TIP: Be sure that early readers have access to print as well as digital books. Arrange for at school pickup of books for children to use in small group, too.

Ask yourself these questions when looking for text at Levels D through I:

- Does this text look interesting to the children in my class (e.g., personal interests, cultural identities, age appropriateness, etc.)?

- Does this book make sense (some decodables really don't)?

- Do the pictures support meaning of this text?

- Does this book match what your students need to practice (e.g., a phonics pattern, high-frequency words, reading in phrases, reading dialogue, or paying attention to new vocabulary)?

- Are you giving kids a balance of fiction and nonfiction text to read?

- Are you exposing children to a variety of texts from a variety of publishers (each company's books will have their own look and feel)?

- Are your students reading books (or just passages)?

- Are you giving your children opportunities to read digital and print versions of text?

- Are you selecting texts that represent the students in your care? Are the characters diverse and their stories relatable?

ONLINE LEARNING TIP: Use screen sharing to model how to access digital readers before the lesson. Send communication to the families on what to have ready for a small group lesson before it begins.

EL TIP: Does this book have things your second-language learners can relate to or know? Do they have or can they easily learn words to talk about this topic or these characters using social language?

Books at level D (left) and level I (right) show how text changes at the early reader stage.

Lesson Plan Format
for Early Readers

at Levels D Through I

Meet with your small groups for children reading at Levels D through I for about twenty minutes. By the end of the early reader stage, students will be reading longer texts with more print on each page. You might have kids "read to the staple" in one lesson. It's okay to divide the book into parts and have kids read it over two or more days. Ask them to think back to what they read the last time before starting a new part of the book.

ONLINE LEARNING TIP: Use a timer when kids are reading in online small groups, too. Start the timer as soon as everyone is logged in.

EL TIP: If there are many new words for multilingual learners, read just a few pages per small group and use the rest of the time to develop language. Have kids talk about the pictures and share their understanding, connections, and questions.

Time is limited in small groups, so choose a phonics, comprehension, fluency, or vocabulary focus, based on students' needs, that will propel your students forward as readers. Look at the Key Reading Behaviors for Early Readers chart (in the online companion, **resources.corwin.com/simplysmallgroups**) to choose reading behaviors to focus on in small group lessons. Work with one or two of these reading behaviors at a time in small group. And remember to include comprehension in *every* lesson!

Use a matching Focus Board with visuals for each lesson to help students know what to pay attention to. You might use the same focus for multiple lessons until you see children using that strategy or skill consistently. There's a space on the lesson plan form for your Focus Board idea.

Use the matching printable Focus Board with visuals in the online companion for inspiration (**resources.corwin.com/simplysmallgroups**). Remind students to use today's focus as they read in small group.

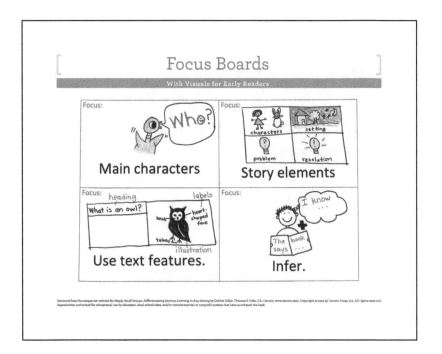

ONLINE LEARNING TIP: Use a Focus Board with visuals online, too. Post your focus on a dry erase board behind you or create a slide with the focus to share. Include the focus in the communication you send with the link to the text kids will read in small group each day.

EL TIP: Add a visual to the Focus Board to help multilingual learners remember what you want them to do as readers or writers.

Here are suggestions for what to include in a small group reading lesson for children reading at the early reader stage. Numbers of minutes are included to give you an idea of how to balance your time during small group. Be flexible and make each session work for you and your students. A printable template for planning is available in the online companion at **resources.corwin.com/ simplysmallgroups**.

WHEN WORKING WITH STUDENTS AT THE EARLY READER STAGE (LEVELS D THROUGH I), INCLUDE THE FOLLOWING IN A SMALL GROUP FOR READING:

Key Reading Behavior Focus Work (warmup) Phonics/phonological awareness lesson (two to three minutes) High-frequency word work (for groups that need this; one minute) Reminder of today's focus (two to three minutes)	• Do phonics work matching the level kids are on and that they will need in the book they are reading. Be sure they have phonological awareness first. • Kids might use letter tiles or Elkonin boxes to make one-syllable words. Use dry erase materials for multisyllable words. • Practice with high-frequency words needed for the book children will read to help these words "stick." Use magnetic letters or dry erase materials. • Use flashcards for or play a quick game with these words, having kids read (and possibly write) each word a few times. • Use a reading Focus Board with visuals. Show students what you expect them to do as readers today. It might relate to phonics, fluency, or vocabulary, depending on their needs.
Book introduction before reading (two minutes)	• Do a brief book introduction. Have kids read the title and think about what the book will be about. Set the purpose and ask or tell them what they will read to find out.
My notes during reading (five to ten minutes)	• Give kids sticky notes to jot down something you want them to pay attention to (e.g., a connection, a question, a new fact). • Listen to individuals and prompt while others read on their own. • Have students read on their own in a quiet voice (or silently at Levels H through I). This is *not* choral or round-robin reading.
Discussion questions after reading (three to five minutes)	• Pre-plan several comprehension questions. Include at least one higher-level question. • Discuss what kids read. Start with what you asked them to read to find out. • Have students share what they tried related to the reading behavior focus (e.g., find a word with the phonics pattern, read a bit of dialogue with expression, show a new word they learned and tell what it means). • Remind kids to keep using that reading focus as they read throughout the day.

(Continued)

WHEN WORKING WITH STUDENTS AT THE EARLY READER STAGE (LEVELS D THROUGH I), INCLUDE THE FOLLOWING IN A SMALL GROUP FOR READING:

In the **next lesson** . . .	• If the book is long and kids only read part of it, review what they read the day before. Then have them repeat the lesson steps as they read the next part of the book. Stick with the same reading behavior focus if that is what readers need.
	• If they finished the book, you might do a small group writing lesson the next time these kids meet.

TIPS for READING WITH CHILDREN in SMALL GROUPS

1. Have students unmute themselves if possible.

2. Before reading, teach them how to take turns talking about the book.

3. During reading, place all but one student in the waiting room to read on their own. Listen to that child read and confer for a minute or so.

4. Then place that student in a waiting room while you bring another child into your meeting space to confer. Try to meet with as many students as you can. Keep it brief.

5. After reading, encourage kids to take turns talking about the book. Then have them show how they used the instructional focus from today's small group lesson.

Small Group Writing Lesson

Some teachers have kids read a book for a day or two, then follow with a writing lesson around the same text. This can help children apply phonics as they make connections and transfer them to spelling. For example, if kids are working on word endings (*s, ed, ing*), help that group create a text where they write a response using words with those endings. You can download a small group writing lesson plan template, pictured on page 106, from the online companion, **resources.corwin.com/simplysmallgroups**.

Small Group Reading Lesson Plan
for Early Readers, Levels D–I

Group: purple   **Date:** March 5

Book Title: *The Class Pet*   **Level:** E

Warm-Up

Key Reading Behavior Focus Work: (review phonics from previous reading lesson)

Phonics/Phonological Awareness:

Contractions: *I'll, that's* (use a rubber band to stretch *I will*)

Write *I will* on the Focus Board. Cover up *wi* with a sticky note and draw an apostrophe.

High-Frequency Word Work:

would, could, said: build with magnetic letters. Have kids change one letter to make *would* become *could*. Highlight *ai* in *said*. Tell kids they must remember the different spelling of *short e* in the word, *said.*

Today's Focus:

Find a contraction in your book. Read it as one word.

> **Focus Board Idea**
>
> Focus:
>
> **I ' ll**
>
> Contractions

Before Reading

Book Introduction

Kate and Kat want to help their class solve a problem. What do you think the problem is? Read to find the problem and resolution.

(Have kids look at the cover and page through the book. Look at page 8 [picture of chart]. Discuss "break.")

During Reading

My Notes

After Reading

Discussion Questions

1. What problem did the class have?   .

2. What was the resolution?

3. Can you think of another way to solve the problem?

In the **next lesson** . . .

Small Group Reading Lesson Plan
for Early Readers, Levels D–I

Group: purple   **Date:** March 6   **Level:** E

Title or book to reread: *The Class Pet*

Key Reading Behavior Focus (to review): reading contractions

Key Reading Behavior Focus Work (warmup repeated from small group reading lesson)

Phonics/Phonological Awareness:

Contractions (I'll); ask kids for others

High-Frequency Word Work:

Build quickly with magnetic letters: *could*, *would*, *said*

*remind about today's focus: sometimes we use contractions to shrink two words

> **Focus Board Idea**
>
> Focus:
>
> **I ' ll**
>
> Contractions

Reread (before writing)

The Class Pet

What we will write:

Pretend we were in Kat and Kate's class. Let's all add a page to the story with our name in it (e.g., "I'll feed the fish," said Jon.).

How we will write:

Each child writes on their own on a dry erase board.

My Notes (during writing)

Sharing (after writing)

First, decide on what the group will write. There are a few options to choose from. You can share the pen and write together with each student contributing a word or part of a word to the message. Or individual students can write their own messages with your support. The children can come up with something they will all write together. Or each child might create a personal response. Vary the writing experience to keep it interesting.

Here are examples of the kinds of writing your small group might do in response to a text read:

- A sentence or two describing the main character (e.g., *Fat Cat looked for a mouse to eat. Kitty Cat got in the way.*)

- A sentence about the setting and its importance in the story (e.g., *The setting of this story is a school. That's why a teacher and his students are the main characters.*)

- Add another page to the end of the book (e.g., *Emma put her tooth under her pillow. In the morning she got a dollar.*)

- A lesson learned from a book (e.g., *Sometimes it's good to be happy where you are.*)

- The plot of a story (e.g., *The fox wanted to eat the sheep. Max rolled on the ground and looked big. The fox got scared and ran away.*)

- A list of animals in a nonfiction book (e.g., spider, moth, bird, dragonfly, earwig)

- A sentence naming another place that might be in the book (e.g., *We like ice cream in the classroom.*)

- A fact from an informational text (e.g., *We will recycle so our trash doesn't end up in a landfill.*)

- The central idea of an informational text (e.g., *Football is played in America and around the world. Fans love the excitement of the sport.*)

- A definition of a new vocabulary word from an informational text (e.g., *When water gets **polluted**, it is dirty and can make people and animals sick.*)

Don't worry if your students can't spell all the words in the writing they plan to do. This is a perfect opportunity to pinpoint phonics needs! Pay attention to what kids are using but confusing. For example, if a student writes *fone* for *phone*, you'll want to help the child learn that the */f/* sound can be represented by *ph* in this word. Have children stretch out the words and listen to the sounds in order. Have them count the sounds and think about which letters represent the sounds. Tell them to also close their eyes and think about what the word looks like in a book. They might use the book as a reference to check their spelling, too. If you are working on a phonics pattern, review that pattern and remind kids to think about its spelling as they write their words.

After children write, spend a few minutes having them share their writing with the group. Teach kids to give compliments to each other first. Then ask them to look at the spellings related to the phonics patterns you're working on. You might have kids use a colored pencil to circle that pattern in the writing they did. Remind them to keep thinking about that pattern as they read and write throughout the day.

ONLINE LEARNING TIP: Nearpod and Google Slides allow you to see students' work as they're completing it so you can monitor their writing live. A shared Google Doc or interactive whiteboard can help with this, too.

The rest of this section contains specific suggestions for focus work related to key reading behaviors for early readers. Here's how to use this information simply to plan and teach in small groups.

1. Start with **phonics and phonological awareness focus work**, which is critical at this stage. These suggestions can help you design small group warmups that will move your students forward as they learn to decode.

2. Then look at **fluency and high-frequency word focus work**. There are suggestions throughout this section for teaching high-frequency words. Knowing these words will help your children become fluent readers. You'll also find ideas for helping early readers develop oral reading fluency, an important bridge to comprehension.

3. Finally, think about **comprehension** and **vocabulary focus work**. Be sure to include comprehension in every lesson! It is why we read. As students progress through higher reading levels, they will encounter new vocabulary. Understanding new words impacts comprehension, so help students pay attention to and use these new words.

Choose Matching Phonics *and* Phonological Awareness Focus Work

Phonics is vital at the early reading stage, no matter the age of the learner. Phonics involves the associations between sounds and how they are represented in print. Phonics understanding enables children to decode words quickly and easily, which leads to greater fluency and enables the brain to better comprehend. I've created a chart of helpful phonics terms with definitions that can be found in the online companion at **resources.corwin .com/simplysmallgroups**.

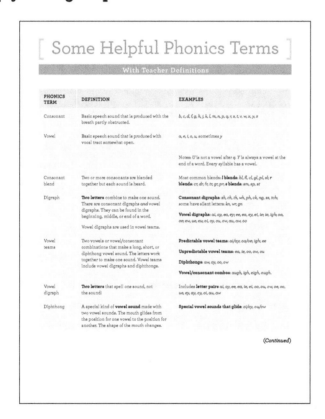

[Some Helpful Phonics Terms]

With Teacher Definitions

PHONICS TERM	DEFINITION	EXAMPLES
Consonant	Basic speech sound that is produced with the breath partly obstructed.	*b, c, d, f, g, h, j, k, l, m, n, p, q, r, s, t, v, w, x, y, z*
Vowel	Basic speech sound that is produced with vocal tract somewhat open.	*a, e, i, o, u,* sometimes *y*
		Notes: *U* is not a vowel after *q. Y* is always a vowel at the end of a word. Every syllable has a vowel.
Consonant blend	Two or more consonants are blended together but each sound is heard.	Most common blends: **l blends:** *bl, fl, cl, gl, pl, sl;* **r blends:** *cr, dr, fr, tr, gr, pr;* **s blends:** *sm, sp, st*
Digraph	**Two letters** combine to make one sound. There are consonant digraphs *and* vowel digraphs. They can be found in the beginning, middle, or end of a word. Vowel digraphs are used in vowel teams.	**Consonant digraphs:** *sh, ch, th, wh, ph, ck, ng, ss, tch;* some have silent letters: *kn, wr, gn* **Vowel digraphs:** *ai, ay, ea, ey; ee, ea, ey, ei, ie; ie, igh; oa, oe; ew, ue, eu; oi, oy, ou, ow, au, aw, oo*
Vowel teams	Two vowels or vowel/consonant combinations that make a long, short, or diphthong vowel sound. The letters work together to make one sound. Vowel teams include vowel digraphs and diphthongs.	**Predictable vowel teams:** *ai/ay, oa/oe; igh; ee* **Unpredictable vowel teams:** *ea, ie, oo, ow, ou* **Diphthongs:** *aw, oy, oo, ow* **Vowel/consonant combos:** *augh, igh, eigh, ough.*
Vowel digraph	**Two letters** that spell one sound, not the sound!	Includes **letter pairs** *ai, ay, ea, ie, ei, oo, ou, ow, oe, oo, ue, ey, ay, oy, oi, ou, aw*
Diphthong	A special kind of **vowel sound** made with two vowel sounds. The mouth glides from the position for one vowel to the position for another. The shape of the mouth changes.	**Special vowel sounds that glide:** *oi/oy, ou/ow*

(Continued)

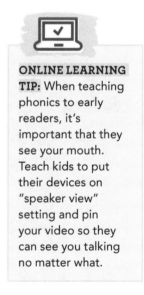

ONLINE LEARNING TIP: When teaching phonics to early readers, it's important that they see your mouth. Teach kids to put their devices on "speaker view" setting and pin your video so they can see you talking no matter what.

Research support is strong for a systematic phonics program. There should be a planned, sequential set of phonics elements that are taught explicitly and methodically. If children develop a strong foundation of phonics at this stage, combined with oral language, they will have an easier time decoding longer words at later stages.

EL TIP: Speech sounds differ among languages. Remind children to look at your mouth as you model how to make new sounds to match letters. If masks are required, wear a face shield during small group so children can see your mouth. You might give each child a small mirror to look at their mouths while making new speech sounds.

Be sure students have **phonological awareness** before adding print. Children should be able to recognize and manipulate *sounds* within words they hear *before* they do this with letters. See pages 72–80 in Section 2 for more information.

And remember to include **comprehension** *with* phonics and decoding words. If meaning is ignored, you will have a bunch of word callers who can say words without any idea of what they've read. You'll find several suggestions for ongoing comprehension work later in this section.

Use the chart that follows to help you plan for phonics and related phonological awareness skills work that will accelerate or propel early readers forward. After examining the *what* and *why*, you'll find the *how* for these important foundational skills, level by level.

PHONICS TO FOCUS ON AT EARLY LEVELS (D–I)	PHONOLOGICAL AWARENESS NEEDED	WHY?
Blends and digraphs in one-syllable words (***fl****-ag*, ***sh****-ip*)	Blend onset and rime in one-syllable words that have blends and digraphs. Teacher gives sounds and kids blend them to say the word.	If kids can't hear the sounds without print, it will be difficult for them to blend the sounds *with* print.
Long vowel patterns, starting with CVCe in one-syllable words (***cake****, **bone***, *mine*)	Hear the difference between short and long vowel sounds. (What is the vowel sound in *cake*?) Do picture sorts of objects representing one-syllable words for one vowel at a time. Kids sort into short *a* or long *a* sound.	If children can't hear the difference between long and short vowel sounds, they may have difficulty choosing the correct vowel sound when decoding.

PHONICS TO FOCUS ON AT EARLY LEVELS (D–I)	PHONOLOGICAL AWARENESS NEEDED	WHY?
Common word endings (*y, ing, ed, es*)	Hear the ending sound of a word. Teacher says a word and kids say just the ending.	If students can't hear or don't use ending sounds in oral language, they may omit endings from words while reading.
Vowel + r (*ar; er, ir, and ur; or*)	Recognize and say the /er/ sound in words. Have kids clap syllables and say the sounds of words with -*er* (*teach-er, moth-er, dri-ver*).	If children have trouble hearing and saying this sound, they may have difficulty decoding it.
oo, ou, ow	Have kids blend sounds in words with this sound (*l-oo-k, m-ou-th, s-n-ow*).	If kids have trouble hearing and blending this sound in words, they may also have difficulty decoding it.
Contractions (*don't, can't, he's*)	Identify these as individual words in a sentence. Teacher says a sentence with one of these words, and kids count how many words.	Contractions should be in oral language before children recognize them in print.
Compound words (*baseball, fireman*)	Hear the two words within a spoken compound word. Teacher says compound word and the child chops it up by syllable and then blends it together again.	If children have trouble hearing and blending these words without print, they may have trouble decoding them.
Syllable types (closed and open syllables)	Hear and blend syllables in a word. Teacher says a multisyllable word and child chops it up by syllable and then blends it together again.	If students have difficulty hearing and blending syllables with no print, they may have trouble decoding them.

As you plan small group lessons, here are some ideas to help you accelerate your students in specific areas.

Phonics Focus Work

Before students at the early reading levels read a new book, many will need a phonics focus lesson. Keep these short and don't include too much.

While listening to individuals read during a small group, prompt children to use the phonics patterns being studied. Try not to correct every decoding error kids make. Your role should be to help children use what they already know how to do as readers. If you notice students pausing or getting stuck, try one of the following depending on the situation:

EL TIP: Be aware that not all languages have vowels. For example, Chinese is made of glyphs, and Arabic uses only consonants. If a student's home language doesn't have vowels, you will have to teach this major difference in English.

- You stopped. Is it making sense?

- Rereading is smart. When you don't understand what you've read, go back and read it again.

- You know _____ (write a related word). Use what you know to figure out this new word.

- What's the vowel sound? Blend the sounds in order. Does that word make sense?

- Flip it. Try the other sound (e.g., /c/ or /g/ or a confusing vowel).

- Find the vowels. How many syllables? Read each part. Blend the parts together.

- What was the tricky word? Why did you skip it?

Here are a few important considerations when doing phonics focus work with early readers:

- Be sure students have phonological awareness before working with each phonics element. See Section 2, starting on page 72.

- Have children look at the words (and not at you) while reading.

- Do some isolated phonics work with the skill kids will need while reading the text *before* they read. But don't have them decode all the new words ahead of time. Leave some decoding work for students to do while reading.

- Use mini anchor charts to remind children of the phonics sounds they will be using as they read.

- Continue to work with phonics elements from prior levels, especially as words get longer.

- Teach syllable patterns, one at a time. Start with one-syllable words, then two-syllable, followed by three-syllable as readers progress through this stage.

Use the phonics-focused teaching tips in the boxes that follow that match the levels of your early readers. Be intentional about which phonics and matching phonological awareness you teach to accelerate student learning.

EL TIP: Contractions may strike fear into the hearts of multilingual learners. Apostrophes are new, so teach their purpose. Write two words that convert to a contraction on a dry erase board. Take turns with kids covering the letters that the apostrophe replaces with a small card showing an apostrophe.

LEVELS D AND E PHONICS FOCUS TEACHING TIPS

- Continue to work with consonant blends and digraphs along with short vowels to help kids decode CVCC and CCVC words. Introduce the closed syllable pattern.

- Help students use chunks to read words quickly (e.g., *s-un*; *cl-ock*; *ch-at*). Include word endings (e.g., *ed, ing*).

- Teach long vowel patterns, starting with VCe. Then move into common spellings of long *a*, then long *e*, and so on. Introduce the VC-silent e syllable pattern.

- Help children understand how contractions and compound words work when they are reading books with these kinds of words.

- Don't focus on too many phonics pieces at once in your small group lesson. Focus on what you think your students need a bit of assistance with (e.g., CVCe, word endings, or *ou/ow*).

EL TIP: Multilingual learners may be confused by compound words. They may be able to blend two little words together when decoding, but the meanings may be confusing (e.g., *butterfly, bulldozer, sunflower*). Help students understand the meanings of compound words.

LEVELS F AND G PHONICS FOCUS TEACHING TIPS

- Focus on vowels: long vowel patterns, vowel + r, and vowel digraphs (e.g., *ai, ay, ee, ea*) and diphthongs (two vowels make one sound, such as *oo, ou*).

- Help children apply their knowledge of vowels to words with two or more syllables.

- Introduce syllable patterns one at a time: closed syllables, open syllables, then vowel + r.

- Help students use chunks and syllables to decode long words (e.g., *buck-et, some-day*).

ONLINE LEARNING TIP: Mute students when doing sound work to minimize audio feedback, but read their lips. Ask individuals to unmute, one at a time, to check their understanding of vowel sounds.

LEVELS H AND I PHONICS FOCUS TEACHING TIPS

- There are many vowel patterns for students to learn.

- As they continue to work with vowels, help children apply this knowledge to words with two or more syllables.

- Help students use syllables to decode long words (e.g., *buck-et, some-day*). Keep working with syllable patterns. Introduce final stable syllables.

EL TIP: English learners may learn long vowels faster than short vowels because long vowels say their letter name. Be on the lookout for e/i confusions and help students sort out these differences. Note that silent e is used in some words other than long vowel words (e.g., *come, are, have, circle*).

Following are photos of some small group phonics warmup ideas. Grab some simple materials—Elkonin boxes (printable available in the online companion), picture cards, and dry erase boards and markers, and get started! Find the focus in bold that matches what your students need in the book they will read today and in upcoming books. Help students practice in isolation for a few minutes and then apply this in the books they are reading.

ONLINE LEARNING TIP: Make your own virtual Elkonin boxes for kids to use in a Google Doc. Then share your screen and allow students to take turns using the annotate tool to fill in the letters.

Kids work with **blends and digraphs** using a laminated Elkonin box. Show a picture of a one-syllable object with a blend or digraph (e.g., *stop, flag, fish, sled, stick*). Students push and say each sound in order. Then they write the letter to represent each sound in order and read the word. Before reading, have them find words with a blend or digraph in their books.

To teach **CVCe,** have kids listen to a one-syllable word (e.g., *cap, slim, bit, rat, tub, mop*) and hold up a finger for each sound. Then they say the vowel sound and tell if it's short or long. Repeat and have them write the word with dry erase. Then have them add *e* in red to the end of the word and read the new word. Make a *bossy e* anchor chart to remember this pattern.

EL TIP: Learning blends helps newcomers pronounce and spell new words in English. These chunks are useful when reading or writing words. Start with *s* blends (e.g., *st, sp, sl, sw*), because these may be easier for multilingual learners to say and read than *l* (e.g., *pl, bl, fl*) or *r* (*br, cr, fr, gr*) blends.

Make **Vowel Teams** anchor charts with students. Write vowels in red and add an exemplar with a photo to help kids remember the sounds of these two-vowel combos. Have kids read blending lines of words using the pattern you're teaching. (See the sample photo.) Then have them look for words with that vowel team in their books before reading.

Sing a bossy r song, such as the one by Jack Hartmann. Make an anchor chart for each **vowel + r** combo as you teach it, starting with *ar*. In later lessons mover to *er*, *ir*, and *ur*. Teach *or*, *ore*, *oar* last. Again, write vowels in red to draw attention to them. Use blending lines to have kids read words with the focus pattern. An example for *ar* is pictured.

Say *I am* while stretching a rubber band. Then let it contract while saying *I'm*. Write *I am* on a dry erase board. Cover up letters the apostrophe takes the place of with a small card. Write *I'm* under it, and tell kids it's called a **contraction** and is used to shrink what is said. Model with several other words (*don't*, *it's*, *wouldn't*). Then have students find and read contractions in their books and tell the two words the contraction shortened.

Tell children that combining two small words can make a **compound word**. Let them manipulate cards to make new words, as shown. Then write some compound words on a dry erase board and ask students to circle the little words. Have them talk about the words using the sentence stem each time they see a compound word. Ask them to be on the lookout for these words as they read.

ONLINE LEARNING TIP: If you don't have a dry erase board to model on during online learning, use a document camera and a piece of paper.

Work with two-syllable words as you teach a **syllable pattern** (e.g., closed syllables). Say words and have kids clap and count syllables, then read nonsense syllables, then mark vowels in a word from the book with red dots. Make an anchor chart for each syllable pattern as you teach it. Remind kids to put their finger under each vowel when they come to a long word to think about patterns and then blend the syllables.

Choose Matching Fluency *and* High-Frequency Word Focus Work

Fluency is a bridge between phonics and comprehension. When readers can decode or recognize words automatically, their brains are free to think about what they are reading. Knowing high-frequency words is a part of fluent reading because as these become sight words, students don't have to work as hard to decode every individual word. Fluency includes reading rate, phrasing, and intonation or expression.

Oral Reading Fluency Work

As they leave the emergent reading stage, students may still point to every word as they read. They were encouraged to do so when they were learning to pay attention to print and may still sound choppy as phonics demands are high. But on repeated readings, fluency will improve.

You might have early readers build fluency by reading nursery rhymes and short poems. This will give them opportunities to read high-frequency words in context. Show and tell them how to move their eyes quickly to the end of a line or to punctuation marks.

Children at the early reading stage are still reading orally. As they subvocalize, they can hear what they're reading, which helps them monitor comprehension. Most children will transition to silent reading at the end of the early reading stage.

Ask children to read in a quiet voice on their own during small group reading. Even though they're reading aloud, encourage them to read on their own instead of having them take turns. Take a minute to lean in and listen to individuals, making note of their oral reading fluency as well as their accuracy.

Pay attention to children's miscues. If they have difficulty decoding words, it affects their fluency. See phonics ideas in the previous section for helping kids with decoding.

After reading, provide opportunities for students to reread parts of the text orally as they discuss what they read. Sharing text evidence improves comprehension *and* oral reading fluency.

Teach early readers to do the following to develop oral reading fluency:

- Decode one- and two-syllable words with ease (see phonics work, starting on page 109)

- Read high-frequency words quickly and easily (see suggestions on the following page)

- Not point to every word with their finger

- Move their eyes quickly across the page rather than stopping on every word

- Pay attention to and use punctuation

Use the fluency-focused teaching tips in the boxes below that match the levels of your early readers. Be intentional about which fluency work you choose in small groups to accelerate student learning.

LEVELS D AND E FLUENCY FOCUS TEACHING TIPS

- Do a high-frequency word warmup before students read in small groups using words they may encounter in that day's book. Ideas are included in the High-Frequency Word Focus Work section that follows.

- Choose text with some words kids already know to build fluency and develop their confidence as readers.

- Remind students not to use their finger to point to every word. Have them use their eyes.

- Have children point out punctuation on a page before reading. Review what to do if you come to a period or question mark. Remind kids to stop at end punctuation.

- Help students notice quotation marks and read those parts in the voice of the character.

LEVELS F AND G FLUENCY FOCUS TEACHING TIPS

- Reading words quickly and easily impacts children's fluency. They might still work with high-frequency words, as needed. Use the Dolch or Fry word list.

- Review the purposes of end punctuation and commas. Work on reading with intonation and expression.

- Model how to move your eyes quickly across the page to read in phrases.

- Help students use their fingers to decode new words, breaking them into chunks or syllables.

- Help students notice quotation marks and read those parts in the characters' voices.

LEVELS H AND I FLUENCY FOCUS TEACHING TIPS

- Review any high-frequency words children are stumbling over.

- Encourage kids to begin silent reading or reading with a quiet voice in their heads. (They may whisper read at first.)

- Review how to read in phrases by moving your eyes quickly across the page to the punctuation. (Use books written in phrases to assist.)

- Help students find dialogue and read in the voices of the characters.

- Find reader's theater scripts for students to practice oral reading fluency.

High-Frequency Word Focus Work

Often lists of high-frequency words are sent home at the beginning of the school year for practice. I recommend limiting the number of words sent home to ten at a time for early readers. After one list is mastered, send home the next.

Section 6 includes a chart of high-frequency words that match early reading levels. There are many words children will need to read quickly and easily! Use this list as a reference and adapt, as needed. Printable lists to send home can be found in the online companion, too, at **resources.corwin.com/simplysmallgroups**.

Here are a few important considerations when doing high-frequency word focus work with early readers:

- Give children practice with the high-frequency words you are teaching in connected text.

- Use poems and nursery rhymes, or books and articles that contain these words.

- Ask kids to highlight high-frequency words and be on the lookout for them, because they are used often!

- Have kids practice with high-frequency word card decks containing a few words they already know and some new ones to build confidence.

Pictured on the next pages are a few quick warmup activities for high-frequency words to use in small group. Limit play to just a minute or so. Then be sure these words are in the new book children will read. You'll find additional ideas for teaching high-frequency words in Section 2, starting on page 67.

Kids **use magnetic letters** or letter tiles to build new words that match today's book. They build one-syllable words on Elkonin boxes, focusing on phonics sounds, and run their finger under the letters to read the word. Then have them mix up the letters and repeat.

ONLINE LEARNING TIP: For free virtual magnetic letters, check out this site: http://www.bigbrownbear.co.uk/letters/

Children **use dry erase materials** to write new words that match today's book. Use Elkonin boxes for one-syllable words to help children focus on sounds and corresponding letters that make those sounds. They run their finger under the word and read it before erasing and repeating. Or ask them to erase sounds as you say them (e.g., /d/, /n/, /ow/).

Play **Our Pile, My Pile** with high-frequency words written on index cards. Use words kids know well with a few new ones added. Place cards facedown and turn them over one at a time. Words kids read quickly go on "our pile." If only one child says it fast, the word goes on "my pile." The goal is to make "our pile" the largest.

Play **Pick Up the Card**. Lay high-frequency word cards on the table, face up. Have multiples of each word. Say a word and see who can pick up that card fast. Ask the group to reread the card after it's picked up. Continue until all the cards are gone. Then have a student lead the game.

ONLINE LEARNING TIP: To play Pick Up the Card online, create a slide with the high-frequency words being studied and screen share it. Put each word in a text box and have kids take turns moving them as they read the words. Call on individuals to find words. Flippity.net might be a useful tool for this, too!

Guess the Word

1. It is on the word wall.

2. It has ▢ letters.
   _{1,2,3,4,5}

3. It starts with ___.

4. It ends with ___.

5. It goes in the sentence _____.

Play **Guess the Word**. Choose a Word Wall word. Students number from 1 to 5 on their own dry erase board. Use the pictured clues, and have kids write a Word Wall word on their boards to guess your word. It's okay if they get it correct on the first try; they will write it four more times! Have them write then read each word as they guess your word. Printable directions, as pictured here, can be found in the online companion.

ONLINE LEARNING TIP: Create a virtual Word Wall using a Google Doc with a 5-x-5 grid. Share this on your screen when playing "Guess the Word" online.

EL TIP: Most high-frequency words don't have much meaning in isolation, so help English learners use these words orally in sentences to help them develop language as well as reading skills.

Choose Matching Comprehension *and* Vocabulary Focus Work

The purpose of reading is to comprehend, so be sure to include this as part of every small group lesson. Remember that vocabulary impacts comprehension. At early levels, many of the words students read will be in their oral language. But as they move across levels, and especially as they read informational text, it will be necessary to learn how to think about new vocabulary to understand what was read.

Be sure students have *listening comprehension* before working on reading comprehension. Most children will develop this during whole group read-aloud and think-aloud time. They should be familiar with story elements, such as characters, setting, and plot (problem and solution or resolution) before working with these in small group.

If children have difficulty with listening comprehension, do a small group read-aloud and pause often, having them articulate what happened so far and what they think will happen next. Have them use the retelling strip available on the online companion to tell what happened in the beginning before moving to the middle, and so on.

Some considerations around comprehension and vocabulary include the following points:

- Plan to have *conversations* with your students before, during, and after reading to develop comprehension and build vocabulary.

- When you give early readers a book in small group, do a brief book introduction *before* they read. Plan a one- or two-sentence summary, such as "Kate and Kat want to help their class solve a problem. What do you think the problem will be?" Then have students look at the cover, read the title, and look through the pictures quickly, as they share their thoughts.

- If needed, orally incorporate new vocabulary as you refer to a picture or two to help students comprehend.

EL TIP: You might work on listening comprehension with second-language learners to build vocabulary and enhance understanding by reading aloud a picture book in small group.

ONLINE LEARNING TIP: Provide extra time when having online discussions. There is a bit of lag time when students unmute and mute their mics again. Ensure students have headphones with microphones to limit background noise.

- Set a purpose for reading, such as "Read to find out what the problem is and how the class solves it" to enhance comprehension.

- *During* reading, lean in and listen to individuals as the rest of the group reads on their own. Take just a minute to talk with each student about what they read to be sure they understood.

- After reading, have another conversation. This time have a short discussion about what students found out as they read.

- Be sure to prompt and share text evidence as well as new vocabulary from the text.

- Plan several discussion questions and include at least one that promotes higher-level thinking.

EL TIP: Multilingual learners often need to spend more time before reading. Have them look at and talk about pictures to build the language needed to comprehend and develop vocabulary.

QUESTIONS to PROMOTE HIGHER-LEVEL THINKING at the EARLY READING STAGE

- Describe the main character. Who else does this remind you of? Why?

- What might have happened if _____?

- Why do you think _____?

- What was the setting? How would the story change if the setting changed to _____?

- What was the problem in the story? Come up with a new problem that could be in the story. How would this change the solution?

- How can you compare and contrast _____ (e.g., two ideas, two text features on this page, two characters)?

- Which text feature helped you better understand this information? How did it help you?

- Why do you think the author wrote this text? What in the text makes you think that?

EL TIP: Having conversations about books builds oral language, which is essential for learning to read and write in a new language. Work to develop social language first. As students progress to higher levels of language acquisition, they can use more academic vocabulary, such as that used in answering higher-level thinking questions.

To help early readers develop comprehension and build vocabulary, encourage them to:

- Pay attention to words more than pictures as they read. Remind them to blend the sounds of a word *and* think about what makes sense, using pictures for support.

- Tell what they think before, during, and after reading. Don't do the thinking for them!

- Make connections to characters, situations, and settings in fiction, and topics or information in nonfiction.

- Make predictions and understand these may change while reading.

- Self-monitor and reread. If they make errors and keep going, remind them to try again.

- Stop and ask themselves what a new word means before reading on.

- Think more deeply. Ask students to tell more or show text evidence.

- Use illustrations and other words around a new word they don't understand.

- Talk about the book using new vocabulary.

Use the comprehension and vocabulary-focused teaching tips in the following boxes that match the levels of your early readers.

EL TIP: Use short video clips to build background knowledge. Make word webs of new words around the topic to develop vocabulary. Have kids listen for those words in the video. They may watch a video more than once.

LEVELS D AND E COMPREHENSION AND VOCABULARY FOCUS TEACHING TIPS

- Teach kids to think about genre—fiction or informational text—when previewing a new book. Help them identify what the book will include (e.g., characters in a story or information in nonfiction).

- Discuss characters and their feelings. Have kids show text evidence using words or illustrations.

- Retell simple beginning, middle, and end of stories.

- Have readers share three facts from informational text.

- Have children show and use new words learned, mostly in informational text.

LEVELS F AND G COMPREHENSION AND VOCABULARY FOCUS TEACHING TIPS

- Genre expands to include simple folktales. Have kids identify genre characteristics (e.g., begins with *Once upon a time*, has three characters, animals talk).

- Ask students to think about the main character and how they interact with other characters in stories.

- Retell with more detail.

- Have readers use what they know with what the text says to make inferences.

- Discuss central or main idea in informational text.

- Teach students to stop if they don't know what a word means. Have them try another word that makes sense there.

- Vocabulary expands, especially in informational text. Help students think about and use these new words when discussing what they learned.

LEVELS H AND I COMPREHENSION AND VOCABULARY FOCUS TEACHING TIPS

- As genres expand to fables and biographies, help students think about the characteristics of these types of texts.

- Move into discussions about characters and their traits. Talk about why they act the way they do. Series books may be available to you and can help kids develop deeper understanding of characters.

- Plots become more developed. Students might use story plot maps to retell.

- Topics become less familiar, so help students think about new information and make connections to it.

- Teach readers to use headings to think about the central or main idea. Have them read text features for additional information.

- Children may use glossaries to help them learn the meanings of bold words.

- Help students use other words around a new word to determine the meaning of new vocabulary.

The photos and captions on the following pages provide suggestions for comprehension and vocabulary focus work in small group. The focus for each activity is in bold.

When reading informational text, teach students to use text features (e.g., table of contents, maps, and diagrams) to determine what the book will be about and **build background knowledge**. Talking in pairs *before* reading helps them tap into what they already know.

Early readers **use sticky notes** to interact with text in a variety of ways: draw an emoji (e.g., smiley, sad face, surprise) to show how they felt when they read a part, write a question mark to show where they wondered about something, or use an exclamation point to show where they really liked something. Or they might use three sticky notes to jot down three things they learned from informational text.

ONLINE LEARNING TIP: Teach online students to use virtual sticky notes like those provided by www.readinga-z.com when reading and interacting with text.

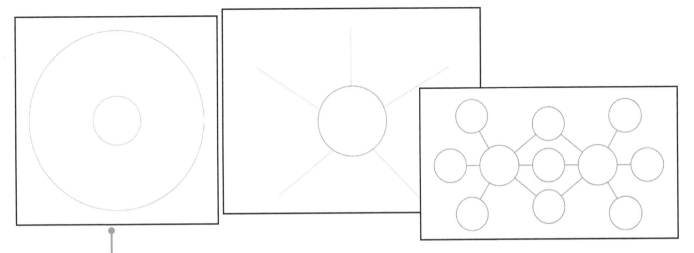

Simple **graphic organizers** used previously in whole group are used by students in small group to construct meaning while reading: circle map for thinking about characters or topics, topic web, or a comparison chart for characters, setting, or information on a topic. Keep the graphics simple so children can draw these on their own.

ONLINE LEARNING TIP: Online groups can use pencil and paper to grow these graphic organizers, too. Ask learners to hold their paper up to the camera so you can see their work. Or your learning management system or a program like Seesaw can allow kids to snap photos of their work to send in.

Children use a **retelling strip** made from colored construction paper to touch and tell major events from a story. Find a printable version in the online companion. Teach with it in whole group and then move it to small group. Include academic vocabulary from your standards for language support.

EL TIP: Have multilingual learners use stick puppets to act out stories when retelling. This makes language learning fun and memorable. Let them use the book for support, too.

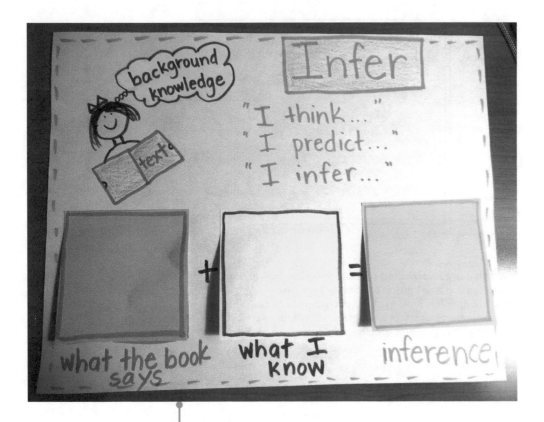

Early readers add sketches and words to show what they know plus what the text says to **make an inference**. Be sure they have learned how to build and tap into background knowledge first. A sample anchor chart is shown, too.

EL TIP: When teaching English learners to infer, you might add this simple language: *It says* (for what the text says), *I say* (for what I know): *So . . .* (this is the inference).

Use an anchor chart that reminds students to stop, look, and think about new word meanings *before* students read a text that has **new vocabulary**. Then give them tape flags to mark places where they stopped to think about a new word. Have them share these *after reading*.

Have kids **choose and illustrate new vocabulary** *after reading* a new text. Write each word with thick black marker on a 3-x-5 card and have children do a quick sketch. Then have them use these words to retell.

If You See This, Try This . . .

It's important to look at what students *can* do. But sometimes there are clear patterns of where children get stuck along a developmental continuum. Here are some specific solutions to common sticking points for early readers.

IF YOU SEE THIS . . .	TRY THIS:
Look at you for approval (instead of looking at the words)	• Tell the student to look at the words. Don't make eye contact, but look at the page, too.
Try to sound out every letter in a word	• Help children read a word using chunks or parts of words. Start with the Most Common Phonograms to Use for Decoding printable available on the online companion. • At Levels F through I, start to teach syllable types (open and closed syllables).
Have trouble with vowel sounds	• Establish a strong foundation of short vowel sounds before moving into long vowels. • Teach kids hand motions to anchor vowel sounds, such as holding an apple for short *a* while saying *a*. • This video from Reading Rockets demonstrates strong short vowel teaching: https://bit.ly/2P3X2h7
Say some of the sounds in a word and make up a word (that may not make sense)	• Coach students to read the sounds. Say, "You're using some of the sounds and making up a word. Stop doing that. Look at the word. Read the sounds (or parts) in order. Be sure the word makes sense."
Finger point to every word on the page and read very choppily	• Help kids transition to using their eyes to read the words instead of finger pointing. There may be too much print on the page. Try a text with fewer lines. Or have students hold a plain bookmark over the text *above* the line they're reading to help with focus.

IF YOU SEE THIS . . .	TRY THIS:
Don't pay attention to punctuation	• Review simple punctuation marks and their purposes. You might have kids use highlighter tape to mark punctuation on a page and practice stopping at these marks.
Read in a monotone voice	• Model how to read a sentence or two with expression. Then have kids echo read to sound like you. You might teach them how to record their reading of a page so they can listen and hear their expression. Or give them a WhisperPhone to hear their voices.
Don't read in phrases	• Use nursery rhymes (or short poems) in small group. Have kids practice reading to the end of the line in a phrase. They might echo read a line or two at a time. Teach them how to record their reading so they can listen to how they sound.
Keep reading even though they don't comprehend	• Set a purpose for reading. • Choose text kids have background knowledge for to aid comprehension. • Students might use sticky notes to interact with the text. See page 128 for ideas.
Decode all (or most) of the words but don't remember what they read	• See suggestions above.
Have difficulty retelling	• Give children a retelling strip to remind them of what to include. See page 267 for ideas. • Have kids read just the beginning then stop and retell. Repeat for the middle. Then have them do the same with the ending.

Section

4

Teaching Transitional Readers

Characteristics *of* Transitional Readers

Students at the *transitional* stage are sometimes referred to as *developing readers*. They are typically in second or third grade but may be in other grade levels. These children can decode most one- and two-syllable words quickly and easily. They are starting to read chapter books and longer informational texts with more print per page. They are reading a wider variety of texts including poetry, graphic novels, simple mysteries, and simple biographies.

Transitional readers are transitioning into silent reading and can read text more fluently. They may get stuck on multisyllable words but are learning to use what they know about vowels and syllable types to decode these words. Likewise, they are paying attention to unfamiliar words and are extending their vocabulary through reading.

Throughout this stage, transitional readers are reading series books and making connections and predictions based on what they've learned about characters and their relationships. These students are also reading and understanding informational text as they build background knowledge about known and new topics. They are learning to use glossaries and other resources to learn specialized vocabulary.

Corresponding guided reading levels are Levels J through M. Many of the changes from one level to the next in the transitional stage center around text length and complexity. Chapters in fiction get longer, as do sections in informational text. Longer parts of a story may be told in dialogue, and children must infer to extract meaning beyond the surface. Illustrations become sparse compared to earlier text levels. Text features expand to maps, diagrams, and insets, and students should learn to use these to gain information about topics they are reading about.

EL TIP: Students learning English as a new language may read at the transitional reader stage in their home language and the early reader stage in their new language. Be sure children have opportunities to grow in both languages.

Transitional Readers and Comprehension

The goal of reading is to make meaning. Continue to read aloud stories, poems, and informational text to transitional readers in whole group. Choose texts with new vocabulary and model how to figure out the meaning of new words. Engage students in discussions about characters and their relationships, sensory images, and new and important information to deepen comprehension. Use your state standards to guide your instruction.

Often students in the transitional stage can decode many of the words in the text as they read independently. But be sure they are also comprehending, especially as you work with them one-on-one and in small group. Readers at this stage may *sound* like fluent readers but still not understand text fully if comprehension isn't expected and inspected.

Help students at this stage talk about what they are reading. Have them participate in small group discussions to deepen comprehension. Ask questions, including those that require higher-level thinking. Because students will be required to take state assessments, also ask questions that use the language of released items from these tests.

EL TIP: Help multilingual learners with the pronunciation of new words. Give students opportunities to read with an online dictionary and click on the mic to hear how to say new words.

When you give transitional readers a book in small group, watch to see what they do first; this may give you a glimpse into their comprehension process. Do they read the title and ponder the cover art, or do they jump into the first page of text without forethought? Help students learn to automatically do the following *before reading* to improve comprehension:

- Look at the cover

- Read the title

- Skim the book, including the table of contents

- Think about genre

Then ask kids to think aloud with you about what they noticed and what they might read to find out. For example:

- "This is fiction. It's a story about a boy and a dog named Henry and Mudge. I will read the first chapter to find out about these characters and their relationship."

- "This is information. I saw many text features and drawings with some photos. I know a lot about space, like the names of the planets. I want to read to find more interesting information about space."

Vocabulary load is higher in the text at transitional levels, so teach students to be on the lookout for new words. Vocabulary affects comprehension, especially at the transitional stage where pictures don't lend the support they did in earlier levels. Help children understand that just because they can decode a word doesn't guarantee that they understand its meaning.

Encourage transitional readers to slow down their reading when they encounter new words and reread to figure out new meanings. Teach them how to use a dictionary. Students might even keep a small notebook to jot down new words during small group and independent reading times. See the Vocabulary Focus Work section on pages 179–188 for ideas of how to help kids learn new words on their own.

ONLINE LEARNING TIP: When reading virtually in small group, teach students how to use drawing tools to highlight new words they are figuring out meanings for.

Fluency also affects comprehension. As kids read words quickly and easily, their brains are free to think about meaning. Most of the words they read are now *sight words*—words they can read rapidly because they have seen them many times. If there are still high-frequency words students stumble over, help individuals work with these. (See pages 166–167 for ideas.)

ONLINE LEARNING TIP: Find digital text with bold words that include hyperlinks. Teach kids how to click on these to find new word meanings.

Start *by* Looking *at* What Students *Can* Do

It's important to meet with students in small groups to build their skills and confidence as readers and writers. And it's more important than ever to plan for acceleration or helping kids advance. Expect students at the transitional reading stage to speak in sentences, especially when working in small groups. Prompt them to tell about the most important parts rather than every detail. If kids speak in more complex sentences, it will affect their writing and encourage them to use more developed vocabulary.

EL TIP: Support multilingual children as they learn to speak in more complex sentences, especially as they acquire more language. Use sentence frames as needed to include academic vocabulary.

Include writing in small group lessons for transitional readers. They might write responses to what they read. Or have them examine books they're reading in small group to look at author's craft such as word choice. Use word hunts to help students learn about vowel and syllable patterns. Remind them also to think about how words look in books when they are trying to spell. The charts that follow can guide you in planning small group instruction based on what you see children are able to do. Use these strengths to help kids accelerate to the next level!

EL TIP: Help multilingual learners examine spellings in the language of instruction and compare it to spelling in their home language.

Transitional Readers May Be Able to . . .

- Have background knowledge for a text before reading

- Use background knowledge to infer

- Identify genre before reading (e.g., story, informational text, poem, drama)

- Know some folktales and fables

- Retell what they read

- Recognize and use text features in short informational text

- Easily decode one- and two-syllable words, especially those with easier vowel patterns

- Clap syllables in words

- Know many high-frequency words

- Reread to fix up words

- Be transitioning to silent reading

- Write longer sentences, often connecting them with the word

- Use letters to represent every sound they hear, including vowels, in longer words

- Spell many one-syllable words correctly

- Try to use vowel patterns but may not use the correct spelling, especially when writing words with more than one syllable

Plan *and* Teach Lessons That Match *the* Development Level *of* Your Students

EL TIP: Break books into even shorter parts for students learning a new language. Look at vocabulary load and plan for kids to read just enough so they comprehend and learn new words from the book in small group.

As you work with students at transitional reading levels, realize that texts at this stage include *more*—more words per page, more complex vocabulary, longer words and sentences, and lengthier sections or chapters. Students are also exposed to new words, new genres, and new cultures in texts at these levels.

Continue to pay attention to children's decoding skills, especially as they encounter words with more than one syllable in the transitional stage. It will be important to teach readers to use syllable types to decode. You may include a bit of phonics work in isolation, but always move that decoding into connected text as well so that children learn to apply those skills. Keep meaning at the forefront and always include comprehension as part of each lesson. Use small group time to help transitional readers become strategic meaning-makers.

MATERIALS NEEDED for SMALL GROUPS at this STAGE

- Fiction and informational texts at Levels J–M

- Reader's theater scripts and poems at transitional levels

- Books in a series at Levels J–M

- Anchor charts for vowel sounds

- Anchor charts with syllable patterns

- Simple graphic organizers for comprehension

- Sticky notes and pencils

- Highlighter tape

- Small whiteboard and plate stand for a Focus Board

MATERIALS NEEDED for ONLINE GROUPS

- Paper and markers (for writing)

- Virtual Word Walls (use a Google Slide with a 5-x-5 table inserted)

- Digital text, including leveled books, books in a series, and articles

- Digital versions of reader's theater and poems

- Interactive whiteboard or a Google Slide for Elkonin boxes

- Drive-through family pickup of materials, including whiteboards and dry erase supplies, leveled and decodable books, simple graphic organizers, and sticky notes

What *to* Look *for in* Transitional Level Text

Choosing the right text for transitional readers is important. You want your students to experience success *and* the joy of reading, especially as they tackle longer texts and new genres. It may be tempting to print or assign passages with comprehension questions but ask yourself if these will promote a *desire* to read. Be sure to read the text before planning and teaching a lesson!

Some other points to keep in mind when choosing texts for transitional readers include:

- Books at Levels J and K are often written in phrases that can help students develop fluency and thus impact comprehension.

- Transitional readers also enjoy reader's theater and poems. As students read dialogue and poetry in phrases using intonation and expression, their comprehension often increases. Use these kinds of text in small group to develop both fluency *and* comprehension.

Ask yourself these questions when looking for text at Levels J through M:

- Will students connect to this text? Is it relevant to them?

- Is this book part of a series? Will it help kids make connections from one text or topic to another?

- Does this book expand the child's world? Does it broaden their horizons and show them cultures, traditions, and experiences beyond those they know? Are these depictions positive?

- Does this book match what your students need to practice (e.g., reading a longer book over multiple days, decoding two- or three-syllable words, reading in phrases, reading dialogue, inferring, or paying attention to new vocabulary)?

- Are you exposing children to a wider variety of genres?

- Are you exposing children to a variety of texts from a variety of publishers (each publisher's books will have their own look and feel)?

- Are kids reading books by a wide variety of authors? Are those authors diverse with authentic voices representative of their cultures?

- Are your students reading books (or just passages)?

- Are you giving your children opportunities to read digital and print versions?

EL TIP: Look for books to use in small groups that represent the culture of your multilingual students. It's a bonus if you can find books with a few words from children's home language, too.

ONLINE LEARNING TIP: Find brief video clips of real footage (not cartoons) to build background knowledge for new informational text topics. Show these *before* kids read in small groups. Share URLs for these clips virtually, so kids can watch them more than once.

Samples of level J (left) and level M (right) books show how text demands increase at the transitional reader stage.

Lesson Plan Format *for* Transitional Readers

at Levels J Through M

Meet with your small groups for children reading at Levels J through M for about twenty minutes. You will want to break the reading of these longer texts into sections just like kids do when they read lengthier books independently. Each time you meet and continue to read a book in small group, ask kids to think back to what they read the last time. They might reread a bit to prompt their memory and orally summarize what they've read so far. Then talk about what they want to find out in the next section.

EL TIP: Vocabulary will affect comprehension, so preview new words and their meanings with multilingual students before they read. Have children act out any verbs while using the words in sentences. Encourage students to talk about the pictures using some of the new words before, during, and after reading.

ONLINE LEARNING TIP: Share links for scheduled small group times and be consistent with days of the week and times. Start and end on time, so students understand expectations.

Time is limited in small groups, so choose a phonics, comprehension, fluency, or vocabulary focus, based on students' needs, that will help your students grow as readers. Use the Key Reading Behaviors for Transitional Readers chart to choose reading behaviors for an instructional focus for each small group. (Printable versions are available in the online companion at **resources .corwin.com/simplysmallgroups**.) Different groups may have a different focus, and this focus will change depending on student progress. Work with one or two of these reading behaviors at a time in each small group. Be sure to include comprehension in *every* lesson.

Use a matching Focus Board for each lesson to help students know what to pay attention to. You might use the same focus for multiple lessons until you see children using that strategy or skill consistently. There's a place on the lesson plan template for your Focus Board idea. See a sample on the next page. Remind students to use today's focus as they read in small group.

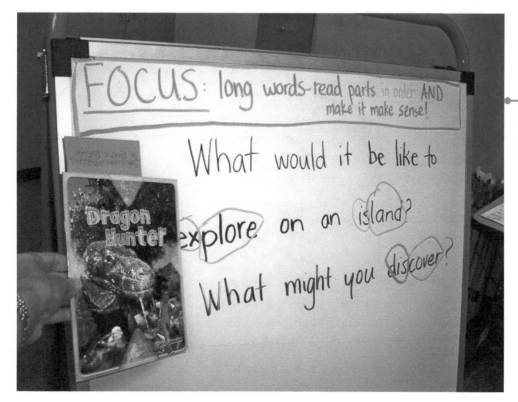

Sample Focus Boards used at transitional reading levels.

ONLINE LEARNING TIP: Include an image of the Focus Board along with the link to the text when you send families the online schedule for the week. Refer to the focus before, during, and after the reading students are online.

EL TIP: Add a visual to the Focus Board to help multilingual learners remember what you want them to do as readers or writers. Ask kids to help you draw something to help them remember what to do.

The chart on the next page shows what to include in a small group reading lesson for children reading at the transitional reader stage. I've included suggested numbers of minutes for each part of the lesson, but please be flexible. Your students may need more time with one part than another. Just be sure they have time to actually read (or write) every time you meet!

Reading behavior to focus on (two to three minutes)	● Use a reading Focus Board. Model what you expect kids to do as readers today. It might relate to phonics, comprehension, fluency, or vocabulary, depending on their needs. Use the Key Reading Behaviors for Transitional Readers chart in the online companion for ideas. Stick with the focus for several lessons.
Before reading (two to three minutes)	● Ask kids what they do first. Be sure they read the title, scan the book and table of contents, identify the genre and accompanying characteristics, and *think* before reading. Have them tell what they will read to find out. Support as needed. ● Indicate how far kids will read (a chapter, a section, several pages) before stopping to discuss the text. You might have them put a sticky note in the book to share where they will stop. ● If students are reading a text over several days, have them reread a bit and summarize what they've read so far. They should preview the next part and set a purpose for reading.
During reading (seven to ten minutes)	● Students at this stage should read silently. Listen to individuals whisper read a bit to you while the others read on their own. Have a brief conversation with each student after you listen to them read to check for comprehension. ● Give kids sticky notes or a simple graphic organizer to jot down something you want them to pay attention to (e.g., character traits, problem, a new fact).
After reading (four to five minutes)	● Discuss what kids read. ● Ask one or two higher-level questions. Use the language of released state tests if you have access to these. ● Have students share what they tried related to the reading behavior focus (e.g., find a word with the phonics pattern, read a bit of dialogue with expression, show a new word they learned and tell what it means). ● Remind kids to keep using that reading focus as they read throughout the day.
In the next lesson …	● If the book is long and kids only read part of it, review what they read previously. Then have them repeat the lesson steps as they read the next part of the book. Stick with the same reading behavior focus if that is what readers need. ● If they finished the book, you might do a small group writing lesson the next time these kids meet. See ideas on the following pages.

Small Group Reading Lesson Plan
Levels J and Up

Group: yellow

Book Title: *Seed Surprises*

Date: January 29

Level: M

Warm-Up	**Key Reading Behavior Focus Work** ⟨phonics⟩ fluency comprehension vocabulary Vowel + r Review sounds of /ar/, /er/, /ir/, /ur/, and /or/ on Focus Board. Use anchor chart. Use blending lines for *er*, *ir*, and *ur*. Write the word *pitcher*. Have kids read it and act out what this word means. In the book, *pitcher* means something you pour with. Repeat with *propeller*. Write the word *hinge*, and have kids read and act it out. Show the door hinge. A door hinge attaches the door to the frame. Tell students they will read words in today's book with vowel + *r*. Be on the lookout! *remind about today's focus **Focus Board Idea** Focus: [ar] [er] [ir] [ur] [or] Vowel + r
Before Reading	**Book Introduction** Have students look at the cover and page quickly through the book. Ask: *What will this book be about? How do you know? Is it fiction or nonfiction? How do you know? What do you want to find out?* Tell them *This book has information about seeds and how they grow. Find three new things you didn't know about seeds. I'll give you three sticky notes to write down that information.* Tell students to also read to find out how seeds spread.
During Reading	**My Notes**
After Reading	**Discussion Questions** 1. What interesting information did you learn about seeds as you read (kids share what they wrote on their sticky notes)? 2. What helps seeds spread? 3. Compare two seeds from this book. How were they the same? How were they different?
Follow-Up Lesson	**Respond to Text in Writing** What we will write: A response: central idea of an informational text with supporting ideas How we will write: Partner writing: two kids work together to write a response or **Look at Author's Craft** word choice organization graphic

EL TIP: Kids learning a new language may have to still subvocalize or hear themselves reading aloud quietly. They may take a bit longer to read silently because they are listening to the language to process it.

TIPS for READING WITH CHILDREN IN SMALL GROUPS

1. Have students unmute their mics if possible.

2. Before reading, teach them how to take turns talking about the book.

3. During reading, place all but one student in the waiting room to read on their own. Listen to that child read and confer for a minute or so.

4. Then place that student in a waiting room while you bring another child into your meeting space to confer. Try to meet with as many students as you can. Keep it brief.

5. After reading, encourage kids to take turns talking about the book. Then have them show how they used the instructional focus from today's small group lesson.

Small Group Writing Lesson

When students have completed reading a book, you might lead a writing lesson around the same text in the next lesson. This can help children apply phonics as they make connections and transfer them to spelling. For example, if a small group is working on decoding multisyllable words, help children create a text where they write a response using a few longer words. Encourage them to use new vocabulary from the text as they write, too.

Response writing is a standard in most states. If a small group has been focusing on thinking about characters and their interactions, then have them choose and write about the interactions between two characters from their recent book. Writing a response can help to deepen students' comprehension.

But don't make children write *every* time they read or every time they finish a book. Think about it. Is that what you do as a reader? Probably not! Talking about a book or reading more books are great responses, too.

When planning a small group writing response, think about *what* the kids might write and discuss it with them.

Here are some ideas for writing response:

- Several sentences describing the main characters and their traits or interactions

- A paragraph about the setting and how it changes in a story

- Several sentences stating the theme of a book with text evidence (e.g., *Sometimes it's good to be happy where you are.*)

- A brief summary of the text including main events or important ideas

- Several interesting facts from an informational text

- The central idea of an informational text with supporting ideas

- A definition of a new vocabulary word from an informational text (e.g., *When water gets **polluted**, it is dirty and can make people and animals sick.*)

- An acrostic poem about a character or topic (see the following example)

Mercy Watson

Magnificent pig

Eats hot buttered toast

Really funny adventures

Causes trouble for her family

You'll love this porcine wonder!

Acrostic poem about a character.

EL TIP: Give multilingual students plenty of time to talk about their ideas in small group before having them write. Speaking is a way to rehearse before writing. They may be more comfortable writing as a group or with a partner, so allow this.

Also think about *how* students might write. Vary the writing experience to keep it interesting:

- Interactive writing: Each student contributes a word or phrase to a message you write together

- Independent writing: Each student writes their own message with just a bit of your support

- Partner writing: Two kids work together to write a response

Don't worry if your students can't spell every word correctly in the writing they plan to do. After all, the purpose of writing is to communicate, so we want students always to focus on ideas and content first. Pay attention to the parts they spell correctly and the parts they confuse. Often kids at this stage will have trouble remembering which vowel team to use or what to do at the end of a syllable. They may forget to double a consonant or use *ee* instead of *ea* in a word.

To help students spell longer words, try the following:

1. Have children clap the syllables and write a short line for each syllable.

2. Then have them write one syllable at a time on the lines to spell a longer word.

3. Tell them to think about what that word looks like in a book.

4. They might use the book as a reference to check their spelling, too.

5. If you are working on a phonics pattern, review that pattern and then remind kids to think about its spelling as they write their words.

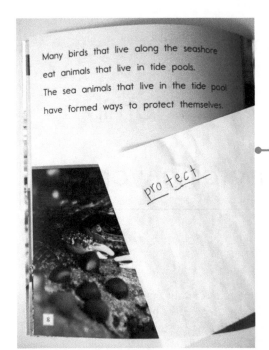

Students write each syllable on a short line to spell a longer word and may use the book read as a reference.

After children write, spend a few minutes having them share their writing with the group. Teach them to compliment each other about their writing. Then look at the spellings related to the phonics patterns you're working on. Students might use a colored pencil to circle that pattern in the writing they did. Remind them to keep thinking about that pattern as they read and write throughout the day.

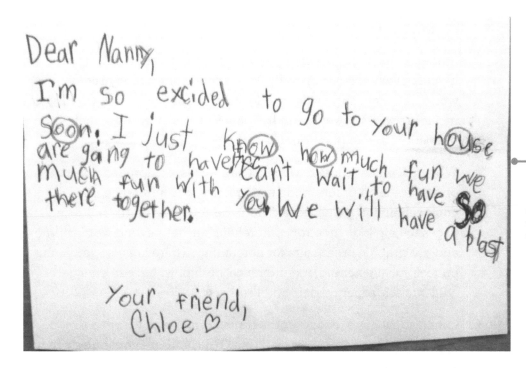

Kids circle the spelling pattern being studied in colored pencil after they write (vowel digraphs in this example).

Another small group writing option is to look at author's craft in the book they just read. Studying someone else's writing can help students strengthen their own writing. Look at students' writing to choose what to focus on and then circle that on the lesson plan template. Choose **word choice** if you want writers to consider using a wider vocabulary or more descriptive words.

Circle **organization** if you notice that children have good ideas but could use help with structure. They might need to work on stronger beginnings or satisfying endings. Or they may have events out of sequence.

Select **graphics** if kids are writing informational text and help them look at text features they might incorporate. Or they may be interested in graphic novels, so examine how authors use illustrations and speech bubbles in these texts. Likewise, have students look closely at illustrations and how illustrators show details related to and beyond the text to create deeper meaning.

Now that you are familiar with transitional readers and planning lessons to meet their needs, let's look at some specific teaching ideas. The rest of this section contains suggestions for instructional focus work related to key reading behaviors for transitional readers. Here's how to use this information simply to plan and teach in small groups.

Think about what each group needs and choose the matching focus. Pick one even if it feels like some kids need all of it immediately! Choose what you think will give them the biggest boost as readers.

1. If you notice that students have difficulty decoding, start with **phonics and phonological awareness focus work**. There are many activities and microlessons on the following pages to help your students move forward in these areas.

2. Students who read in a choppy way, skip punctuation, or sound monotone when reading orally can benefit from **fluency focus work**. There are suggestions following for fluency activities, including working with high-frequency words, phrases, punctuation, intonation, and expression.

3. When you have students who just call words, comprehend only on surface-level points, and need practice with inference, choose **comprehension focus work**. There are activities on the following pages to help kids monitor comprehension, get beyond word calling, and use graphic organizers for notetaking. There are also segments on reciprocal teaching and inference, both of which can engage students as deeper readers and thinkers.

4. Often, you'll have readers at the transitional stage who can decode words but don't know their meaning. This is where **vocabulary focus work** can make a big difference! On the following pages, you'll find a variety of teaching tips and activities to help students develop important vocabulary skills that allow them to progress to the next stage.

Choose Matching Phonics *and* Phonological Awareness Focus Work

Phonics is necessary for students who are learning to read and is still needed at the transitional reading stage. Phonics emphasizes letter–sound relationships. It involves the associations between sounds and how they are represented in print. Phonics understanding helps children decode words quickly and easily, which leads to greater fluency and freeing the brain to better comprehend.

In previous stages, children learned how to represent simple individual speech sounds and then combined these to read chunks. But by the transitional stage, readers encounter many words with more than one syllable and multiple ways to represent speech sounds, especially long vowels.

While reading texts at Levels D through I, children should have learned about vowel patterns (e.g., *ai/ay, oa/oe, igh/ee*, vowel + r) and used these to decode one-syllable words. Now kids must be able to decode multisyllable words with an ever-widening variety of vowel patterns. If students do not have a solid foundation in phonics, they may get stuck in the transitional reader stage. Research shows that students need a planned, sequential set of phonics elements that are taught explicitly and methodically.

By the end of the transitional reading stage, your students should understand syllable types as they learn to decode words with more than one syllable. Directly teach these, one at a time. Syllable types include:

- Closed syllable, which has a short vowel sound and ends in a consonant (e.g., *mit-ten*)

- Open syllable, which ends in a vowel that makes the long sound (e.g., *ba-by*)

- VCe syllable, which ends in a silent *e* making the preceding vowel long (e.g., *race-way*)

- Vowel + r syllable, which ends in vowel plus *r* making that vowel sound (e.g., *stir-ring*)

- Stable final syllable, which has a consonant followed by -le and says /ul/ (e.g., *cas-tle, ta-ble, sim-ple*)

- Vowel teams, which include two vowels or vowel/consonant combinations that make a long, short, or diphthong vowel sound (e.g., *loud/est, need/ed, eight/y*)

Here are sample anchor charts you might use as you teach syllable types.

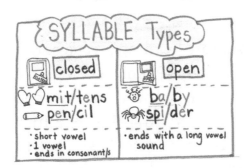

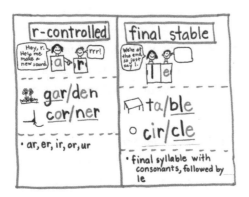
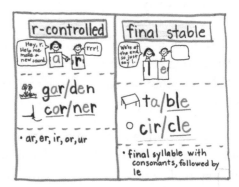

For more information on teaching phonics, I recommend Wiley Blevins's book *A Fresh Look at Phonics* (2016). You might also check out Linda Farrell's videos on reading intervention at www.readingrockets.org. For a list of phonics terms and their definitions, see Some Helpful Phonics Terms in the online companion.

EL TIP: Be aware of the differences between your language of instruction and multilingual students' home language, especially related to sounds and letters that represent those sounds. This information from the website Colorín Colorado may help you understand the differences between Spanish and English sounds: https://bit.ly/3s3rMNP

Phonological awareness, which is based in letter–sound relationships, isn't just for emergent readers. Children should be able to recognize and manipulate *sounds* within words they hear *before* they do this with print. Work with transitional readers on phonological awareness before adding text, especially if they have difficulty decoding multisyllable words. Have students listen and blend syllables with no print before having them read printed multisyllable words. For example, pause between each syllable as you say *"gar-den-er."* Have kids repeat the syllables and blend them to say *gardener.* See pages 72–80 in Section 2 for more information on phonological awareness.

Please use the ideas in this section to help your students in small group instruction. Check out the charts that follow to help you focus phonics instruction (and related phonological awareness) in small groups. And remember to include comprehension *with* phonics and decoding words. If meaning is ignored, you will have a bunch of word callers who can say words without true understanding of what they've read.

EL TIP: English learners need phonological awareness as they learn a new language. Spend time developing this important skill.

PHONICS TO FOCUS ON AT TRANSITIONAL LEVELS (J–M)	PHONOLOGICAL AWARENESS NEEDED	WHY?
Long vowel patterns, including those with more complex spellings in one-syllable words (w**eigh**t, pr**aise**) and later in two-syllable words (n**igh**ttime, del**igh**ted)	Hear the difference between short and long vowel sounds. (What is the vowel sound in *flight*?) If needed, have kids sort pictures of one-syllable objects with the long or short vowel sound for a letter (e.g., *fly, pie, pig, pipe, lips*).	If children can't hear the difference between long and short vowel sounds, they may have difficulty choosing the correct vowel sound when decoding.
Vowel + r (*ar, er, ir, or, ur*) especially in multisyllable words	Recognize and say the *-er* sound in words. Have kids clap syllables and say the sounds of words with *-er* (*teach-er, moth-er, driv-er*). Repeat with other vowel + r combinations.	If children have trouble hearing and saying this sound, they may have difficulty decoding it.

(Continued)

(Continued)

PHONICS TO FOCUS ON AT TRANSITIONAL LEVELS (J–M)	PHONOLOGICAL AWARENESS NEEDED	WHY?
Diphthongs and variant vowels (e.g., *oo, ou, ow, augh*) in one- and two-syllable words	If needed, have kids blend sounds in one-syllable words with this sound (*l-oo-k, m-ou-th, t-augh-t*). Then work on having them blend syllables with these patterns (*look-ing, flow-er, out-doors*).	If kids have trouble hearing and using these sounds in spoken words, they may also have difficulty decoding them.
Common suffixes (*ed, es, ing, ful, ness*)	Hear the ending parts of words. Teacher says a word and kids say just the ending (*rain-ing, ing; beau-ti-ful, ful; hap-pi-ness, ness*).	If students can't hear or don't use ending sounds in oral language, they may omit endings from words while reading.
Common prefixes (*un, re, dis, mis*)	Hear prefixes in words. Teacher says a word and kids say just the prefix (*re-tell, re; pre-view, pre; dis-ap-pear, dis*).	If children can't hear prefixes, they may have trouble reading and understanding the meaning of these words.
Syllable types 1. Closed syllable 2. Open syllable 3. VCe syllable 4. Vowel + r syllable 5. Stable final syllable 6. Vowel teams	Hear and blend syllables in a word. Teacher says a multisyllable word and child chops it up by syllable and then blends it together again.	If students have difficulty hearing and blending syllables with no print, they may have trouble decoding them.

Before students at the transitional reading levels read a new book, some may need a phonics focus lesson. Look at your data and the prior chart to determine which phonics patterns they still need support with. Be sure to read the text before teaching with it and plan for a phonics warmup that matches the needs of that group! Keep these warmups short and don't include too much.

During reading, prompt students to use the phonics patterns reviewed in the warmup. Try not to fix kids' mistakes before they even realize they made them!

But don't let kids keep reading if they are making up words or not paying attention to decoding. Here are some prompts you might use when students make errors:

- You just read _____ . Does that make sense?

- You made up a word using some of the sounds. Stop doing that. Try again and read the sounds in order.

- It's smart to reread. It helps you fix mistakes and understand what you read.

- Find the vowels. How many syllables? Read each syllable in order. Think about what the word means and if it makes sense.

- Use the anchor chart to help you read those vowels.

- What was the tricky word? Why did you skip it? Try it again. I'll help you.

Here are a few important considerations when doing phonics focus work with transitional readers:

EL TIP: Vowel patterns in English can be challenging. Make connections to cognates in Spanish (or French or Italian), so children can see the similarities in these spellings and speech sounds.

LEVELS J–M PHONICS FOCUS TEACHING TIPS

- Have students look at the words (and not at you) while reading.

- Teach syllable types to help kids decode longer words. Create an anchor chart for reference.

- Do some isolated phonics work with the skill kids will need while reading the text *before* they read. But don't have them decode all the new words ahead of time. Leave some decoding work for kids to do while reading.

- Use mini anchor charts to remind children of the phonics sounds or syllable types they will be using as they read.

- Help students use parts, including affixes and syllables to read words accurately. Teach kids to think about affixes to help with word meanings.

- Don't focus on too many phonics pieces at once in your small group lesson. Focus on what you think your students need a bit of assistance with (usually specific vowels or syllables).

- Use word hunts and sorts to help children learn phonics patterns being studied.

EL TIP: Be sure students have phonological awareness before working with syllables. Spanish is taught in syllables, so this should be easier for Spanish-speaking students.

Phonics Work

Before reading a new book, some students may need a phonics focus lesson. Take notes when listening to students read to help you determine which phonics patterns they need to work with. The easiest way to do this with transitional readers is to draw a line and jot down what the child said on top and what the text said below it, as shown in the photo. In the example pictured, the student is confusing some vowel sounds and making up words, especially in longer words. This miscue signals the need to teach how to decode two- and three-syllable words containing open and closed syllables.

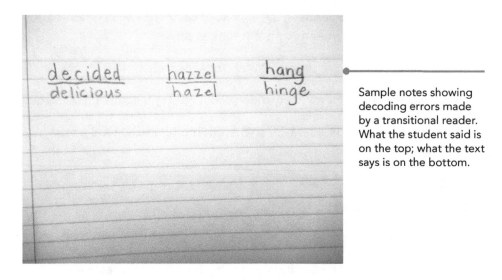

Sample notes showing decoding errors made by a transitional reader. What the student said is on the top; what the text says is on the bottom.

You might notice that some students still need help with phonics patterns that were taught in the early reader stage. Use ideas from previous sections of this book if students have difficulty with the following:

- Decoding blends and digraphs (see pages 114–115)

- CVCe words (see page 115)

- Contractions (see pages 105–106, 116)

- Compound words (see page 117)

Following are photos of small group phonics warmup ideas for students at the transitional stage. Choose the focus in bold that matches your students' needs and then select books with those phonics patterns in which to practice reading. Help students practice in isolation for a few minutes and then apply this in their new book.

her first curl

Review a bossy r song, such as the one by Jack Hartmann. Make or review with an anchor chart for each **vowel + r** combo as you teach it, starting with *ar*. In later lessons mover to *er*, *ir*, and *ur*. Teach *or*, *ore*, and *oar* last. Again, write vowels in red to draw attention to them. Use blending lines to have kids read words with the focus pattern. An example for *er*, *ir*, *ur* is pictured.

[Blending Lines Sample]

for Phonics Patterns, *er, ir, ur*

To create blending use high-utility words. Move from easy to more difficult. Follow these steps:

  Line 1: minimal contrasts (from known to new)

  Line 2: vary initial sound

  Line 3: vary final sound (or another pattern with that sound)

  Line 4: mixed set with target skill

  Line 5: review words

  Lines 6 and 7: connected text

he her chip chirp hut hurt let letter
winter hammer paper father mother
girl bird first burn turn fur
teacher nurse skirt hurry birthday
farm yard sharp yard mark
A bird made a nest with some dog
fur in our yard.
My mother said, "Sunburn hurts!
Use sunscreen first."

EL TIP: English learners may learn long vowels faster than short vowels, since long vowels say their letter names. Help them look carefully at the varying ways to represent long vowels. Start with the most common spelling patterns.

Use the **blending lines** sample to have students practice reading words with a particular phonics pattern. Print a copy (from the online companion) and point to the words in a row, one at a time, while kids read them aloud in unison.

cloud

shoulder

touch   soup

Make **Vowel Teams** anchor charts with students. Write vowels in red and add an exemplar with a photo to help kids remember sounds of these two-vowel combos. Start with predictable vowel teams, such as those for spelling long *a* or long *o*. Have kids read blending lines of words using the pattern you're teaching. (See the sample in the online companion.) Then have them look for words with that vowel team in their books before reading.

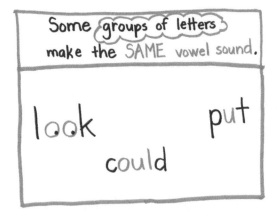

Create **vowel team (diphthong and variant vowel)** anchor charts for the phonics students need to practice and learn, as shown. Play a matching game with word cards containing these patterns. You might use this game from the Florida Center for Reading Research using *ea, au, aw, ow, oa, ai, ay, ee*: https://fla.st/2XG35JS. Tell children to be on the lookout for these phonics patterns in their new book and jot down a few words they find. After reading the new book, share these words.

Prefixes change the meaning of root words.

prefix	meaning	examples
un-	~~not~~	unkind unhappy unlucky
re-	again	replay recycle refresh
non-	~~not~~ or without	nonfiction nonstop nonsense
over-	too much	overcook overdo overpay

Suffixes change the meaning of root words

Suffix	Meaning	Examples
ful	Full of ___.	Cheerful thankful joyful careful
-ly	Tells how Something is done In a ___ way.	Kindly Smoothly quickly lovely slowly
_able	Capable of or able to.	& likeable twistable breakable comfortable loveable
_ness	The state of being ___	Kindness fairness neatness madness Sadness happiness

Create an anchor chart of the most **common prefixes**, as shown. These make up over 95 percent of prefixed words. Then students decode a few words using the new prefixes, as shown, and tell their meanings. Next, they look for words with these prefixes as they read in small group and jot these on a recording sheet. Repeat with the most **common suffixes**, starting with those shown. Add to the charts after kids know these affixes well.

☆

EL TIP: Kids learning a new language often omit endings. If they speak Spanish as their first language, they aren't used to saying (or reading) words with a consonant cluster at the end. That's why they'll say *walk* instead of *walked*. Point out the ways -ed at the end of the word is read (e.g., *helped, wanted, loved*).

How to Decode Long Words

1. **Look for** parts you know.
   Use your fingers **to** chunk.

2. **Look for the** vowels.
   Think about syllable patterns.

3. **Read the** parts in order.

4. **Reread the word in** the sentence.
   Does it make sense?

important

How many vowels? Together or apart? How many syllables?

closed? open? vowel + r?

important

Doing a good job is important.

Teach how to decode long words and make an anchor chart, as shown. Start with two-syllable words as you teach (or review) a **syllable type** (e.g., closed syllables). Then try three- and even four-syllable words. Use a few from the book kids will read. Say words and have kids clap and count syllables; then read nonsense syllables, then mark vowels in a word from the book with red dots. Remind students that every syllable has a vowel. Make an anchor chart for each syllable pattern as you teach it. Remind kids to put their finger under each vowel when they come to a long word to think about patterns and then blend the syllables.

pencil, hammock, running, their names
pic, com, hun, jol

Ask, *How many vowels? Are they together or apart?*
How many syllables?

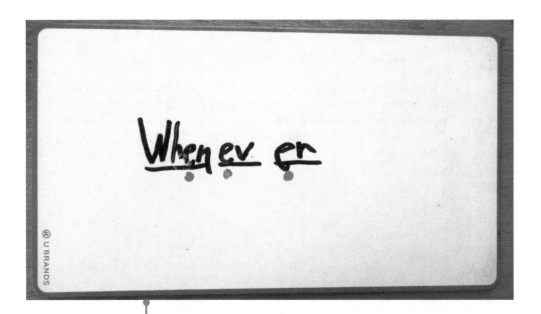

Students use syllable patterns while writing, too. They clap the syllables in a long word, then draw a line for each syllable, remembering that each contains a vowel. Finally, they stretch the sounds of each syllable and **write the long word, one syllable at a time**. They check to be sure each syllable has a vowel.

Choose Matching Fluency Focus Work

Students who have difficulty decoding words quickly and easily will struggle to read fluently. And fluency affects comprehension because when the brain is working to decode, it has less capacity to work on making meaning.

Students at the transitional stage of reading are sometimes unaware of their reading rate or how they sound as readers. Help kids understand *what* fluent reading sounds like to expedite their development in this area. Here are some ideas:

- Teach students to record themselves and listen to their oral reading fluency. They can use the fluency rubric to set specific goals. You'll find a How Fluent Was My Reading? goals sheet in the online companion at **resources.corwin.com/simplysmallgroups**.

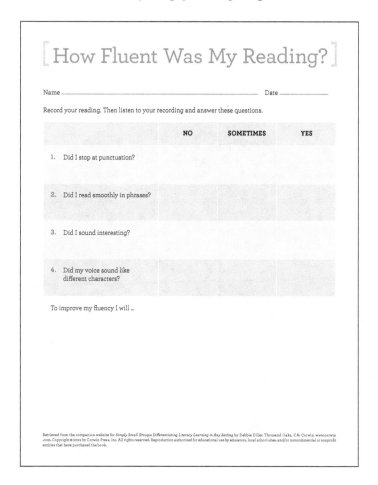

[How Fluent Was My Reading?]

Name _____ Date _____

Record your reading. Then listen to your recording and answer these questions.

	NO	SOMETIMES	YES
1. Did I stop at punctuation?			
2. Did I read smoothly in phrases?			
3. Did I sound interesting?			
4. Did my voice sound like different characters?			

To improve my fluency I will …

- Use a stopwatch in limited doses. Help students set a realistic fluency goal, such as "I will read sixty words per minute" (if they are reading at fifty words per minute, for example). Make a recording where you (or a child) read at the desired rate. Then play the recording so students know what that fluency rate sounds like. Have them record their oral reading and then listen to it. They might time their reading as they listen to the recording (not as they are reading).

- Have kids practice reading familiar text to improve their oral reading fluency rate. Let them reread books from small group.

- Use short text for students to practice and improve their oral reading fluency. Seeing fewer words on a page makes the task less daunting and may improve confidence. Poetry and nursery rhymes work well.

- Some teachers also use a Recording Studio as a literacy station where kids can practice recording and listening to themselves read orally. (Find out more about the Recording Studio station in my book *Simply Stations: Listening and Speaking*.)

Students at the transitional reader stage practice reading familiar text from small group at a Partner Reading station.

Along with helping students become more aware of how they sound as readers, there are many ways you can help students improve their fluency in small group. Here are a few general considerations for teaching for fluency:

LEVELS J–M FLUENCY FOCUS TEACHING TIPS

- Model how to move your eyes quickly across the page rather than stopping on every word as students learn to read silently.

- Remind children to read silently unless you are listening to them read (to check on accuracy and fluency).

- Select easier text for kids to practice fluent oral reading, if needed, to build skill and confidence.

- Consider using reader's theater or poetry in small groups to build fluent oral reading. Students might read aloud different parts to work on reading dialogue with expression.

- Have children point out punctuation on a page before reading. Review what to do if you come to a period or question mark. Remind kids to stop at end punctuation.

- Help students notice quotation marks and read those parts in the voice of the character.

- You might have the music teacher help students make connections to phrasing, too. We read and perform music in phrases to improve its flow.

- Some students may benefit from practicing reading simple phrases. You can find Fry's reading phrases here: https://www.d57.org/Downloads/frys_sight_word_phrases.pdf.

- Review high-frequency words as needed if kids aren't reading them fluently in text.

- If students typically speak slowly or in a nonphrased way, help them with oral language before fluent reading. Try teaching students to record themselves and listen back to hear their speaking and eventually their reading. They may not read faster than they talk.

To read fluently, students must be adept at using the following: **high-frequency words, phrases, punctuation, intonation, and expression.** Listen to children read, and jot notes related to their fluency. Then use ideas from the following pages to plan for differentiation based on students' needs for oral reading fluency.

High-Frequency Word Focus Work

Most students in the transitional stage of reading will probably not need to work on reading high-frequency words. But they may need practice writing these words accurately. Help children at this stage pay attention to words they should be reading *and* writing correctly.

I've included lists of high-frequency words needed at emergent and early reading levels in the online companion at **resources.corwin.com/simplysmallgroups**. Be sure your students know these words before introducing additional high-frequency words. You might consult the Fry or Dolch lists if you would like a reference for other high-frequency words for transitional readers.

Use a black marker to write each high-frequency word children need to practice on a separate plain white 3-x-5 card. Or use the printable cards provided in the online companion (for words kids still need to practice from emergent or early reading levels). Pictured here are a few things to try with these simple materials to help students learn to read and write high-frequency words in small groups.

Play the **Match It/Write It Game**. Hand out an even number of cards to each child. (Be sure that each card has a match.) Kids take turns showing a card and reading it quickly. Whoever has a match, reads the same word and puts their card on top of its match. Then have all students try to write that word on a dry erase board (without looking at the card). Whoever writes the word fastest (and accurately) gets that pair of cards. Play until all cards have been matched. Then kids read their matches as they return the cards to you.

Play **Find It and Write It**. Deal cards evenly. Have each student read their words quickly and then find and read these words in their new (or a familiar) book (or somewhere in the room they can find it quickly and easily). Every time students find a word have them also write it. See who can find the most words.

Play **Color Code the Tricky Part**. Flash a card to the group. Have them read it. Talk about the tricky part of the word and highlight it with colored tape or a marker, as pictured. Then turn the card over and have the kids close their eyes, picturing the word as they say it again. Ask them to write the word from memory on a dry erase board using a different color for the tricky part, then read it, scanning their finger under the word from left to right. Show the card again, have kids check their spelling, and read the word one more time.

Phrases Focus Work

If you have students who read in a choppy, robotic way, teach them to read in phrases. This is also referred to as *prosody*. I often tell kids to "read in phrases so it sounds like you're talking." Try these ideas, as pictured.

Choose **text written in phrases**. Here are some samples. Many books at Levels J and K are formatted this way.

Show and tell children how to **move their eyes quickly** across the page to a punctuation mark to read in phrases. Model by using a pointer or your finger in a fluid scooped motion under the words. This fluency Focus Board serves as a reminder in small group. Use short text with fewer words and lines on the page to start as shown.

Have kids **tap or clap the beat or rhythm** as they read a poem to improve their reading rate.

EL TIP: Have students listen to recorded text before they read it on their own. Having this model of fluent reading may help them read in phrases.

ONLINE LEARNING TIP: Have kids listen to recorded text that has closed captioning. Students can follow along as the reader reads a story in phrases. You might try Storyline Online to get started. Here's a great example: https://www.storylineonline .net/books/missing-carrot-cake/

Punctuation Focus Work

Some transitional readers skip punctuation, especially as they try to read faster. This can impede their oral reading fluency. Help children pay attention to punctuation as it helps both comprehension and fluency. Use the following photos for inspiration.

A **punctuation anchor chart** reminds kids to use these special marks when reading (and writing).

Students **use highlighter tape** to mark a variety of punctuation on a page or two of text. Then they practice reading, paying special attention to how it sounds. Have them read it without punctuation, too, to hear the difference. Then have them read a few more pages, paying attention to punctuation even though it's not highlighted.

Project a sentence or two **without punctuation**, like this example from a favorite children's book, and have kids read it. Then they add punctuation and read it again, comparing how it changes the meaning. *Once upon a time there were three little pigs they were brave they were bold one fine day they set off to see the world.*

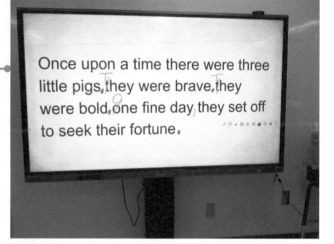

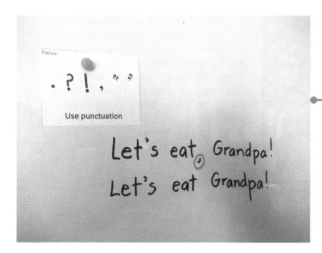

Use sentences where **changing the punctuation** changes the meaning of a sentence. For example, "Let's eat, Grandpa!" means something different than "Let's eat Grandpa!" Here is a website with illustrated examples: https://bit.ly/3qytDcr.

ONLINE LEARNING TIP: Teach learners how to use the annotating tools for highlighting on an e-reader. Have them highlight punctuation on just one page and try reading it with and without punctuation to hear the difference punctuation makes.

Intonation and Expression Focus Work

It's important to read with intonation and expression because it adds meaning to the text, especially when reading orally. Reading in a monotone voice sounds boring and can impede comprehension. To help kids read expressively, try the fluency-focused ideas pictured here.

ONLINE LEARNING TIP: Teach children how to add captions with sound to a piece of informational writing online. They type or write captions and then add a sound recording of that text.

Have students read familiar folktales or fables (books with just two characters) to **read dialogue**. They use a conversation card to think aloud about a character and how he or she feels before reading that part of the dialogue or reader's theater script to add expression.

ONLINE LEARNING TIP: Kids might record a piece of writing they've completed as an audio publication for others to listen to. This adds purpose to reading with intonation and expression.

Transitional readers **make recordings** for other students, including those in younger grades, to use at a Listening and Speaking station. This gives them fluent oral reading practice with purpose. They practice reading with intonation and expression and save their best recording.

Choose Matching Comprehension Work

An important area of focus for many transitional readers is comprehension. You may have students who can decode but can't remember what they've read. Or you may have readers who have difficulty inferring. Vocabulary greatly impacts comprehension, and texts at Levels J–M have many more new words than those preceding them.

Comprehension should be included in *every* small group reading lesson. When done well, this can prevent students from becoming or remaining word callers. It can be helpful to think about comprehension as the thinking work we do *before*, *during*, and *after* reading.

Before students read a new book, do a book introduction to get them thinking about the book. Model how, as proficient readers, we scan the covers and read the inside flap to get an idea of what the book is about. This primes reading comprehension. Have students look at the cover and make predictions. They might even glance quickly through the book. Then tell just a tiny bit of what the book will be about without giving away too much. For example, *This book is about a boy who is scared and runs away.*

Help students set a purpose *before* reading, too. Ask them what they want to read to find out. For example, after previewing a book titled *Earth's Water*, a child might say, *I will read this section to find out something I didn't already know about different forms of water.* This is more helpful than telling kids, *Read the book and we'll talk about it when you're done.* In addition, it may deter children from becoming word callers who read words without thinking about meaning.

As children read on their own *during* the small group reading lesson, check in with individuals to listen to their decoding and fluency. But check their comprehension, too, by asking them about what they have read so far. You might have them tell about interactions and relationships between characters in a story or something new they learned in informational text. Ask them about what they said they wanted to read to find out.

Another way to help kids comprehend is to give them sticky notes to jot something specific *during* their reading. If you asked them to pay attention to character traits, have them write a few words on a sticky note about that character. Or if you want them to infer, have them jot their inference on the sticky note where they made it.

After reading, have a conversation with the group about what they read. Begin with what they read to find out. Encourage them to use text evidence or their sticky notes. Always plan a question or two that gets them to think deeper.

QUESTIONS to PROMOTE HIGHER-LEVEL THINKING at the TRANSITIONAL READING STAGE

- Compare _____ to _____ . How were they the same? How were they different?

- What would have happened if _____?

- What questions would you ask _____ if you could talk to her?

- Why do you think _____?

- What is the theme of this story? What makes you think that?

- What is the relationship between _____ and _____?

- Suppose you could _____ . What would you do _____?

- Predict what might happen if _____ .

- Do you agree with _____? Why or why not?

- What is your opinion of _____?

- Would it be better if _____?

- Why do you think the character _____?

- Based on what you know, how would you explain _____?

- What would you recommend _____?

EL TIP: Take extra time to talk about the cover and the pictures with kids acquiring a new language. Provide support for students to use these new words as they talk about the text. Ask higher-level questions to help students engage in using academic language.

Monitoring Comprehension

Begin by ensuring that children know what *comprehension* means. Don't just talk about comprehension. Explain and show kids that they should *understand* what they read.

Help students develop awareness of their own understanding as they read. Work on self-monitoring, or knowing if you're understanding and fixing it up, and make an anchor chart to remind students to do this. Examples follow.

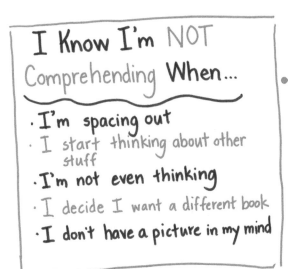

Sample I Know I'm Not Comprehending When . . . anchor chart made with third graders at the start of the year.

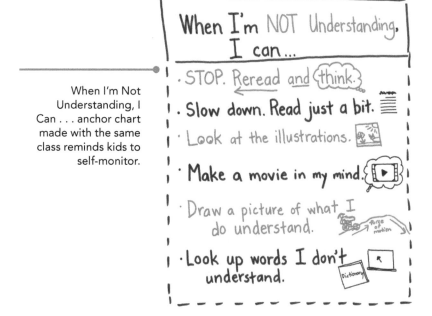

When I'm Not Understanding, I Can . . . anchor chart made with the same class reminds kids to self-monitor.

Solving Word Calling

You may have students who aren't monitoring their reading, but they can decode anything you put in front of them. They're word callers—kids who read all the words correctly but remember little to nothing about what they read. Focus on comprehension, *not* decoding, with these students. When talking with children and their families about their reading needs, be sure to say that these students are *decoding*, not reading, at a certain level. Only call it *reading* when kids are comprehending *and* decoding.

Also be sure students have listening comprehension intact. If students have difficulty with listening comprehension, focus on this in small group by reading stories and informational text to them and helping them discuss what they heard. They might need to jot down simple notes using pictures or a few words to help them visualize.

For children who have developed the habit of reading words without expecting to understand, here are several simple things you can do to improve their comprehension:

- Expect comprehension. Tell students to *think* before, during, and after they read. Model what this looks like as needed.

- Choose texts for small group carefully. Pick books and articles kids *can* comprehend as they read them on their own. Be sure they have interest in and background knowledge for the text to break the word-calling cycle.

- Instead of reading the title to them, ask students what they should do before reading and why. Give *the readers* responsibility. Eventually, they will read the title and use the cover plus background knowledge to predict what the text will be about without you having to prompt them.

- Help kids set a purpose for reading. This helps them focus as they read to find something specific. For example, *I will read to learn who the main character is, what she likes, and how she acts.* Or, *I want to find out about the different kinds of sharks and where they live.*

- Give students an explicit task to help them keep track of their thinking while reading. They might use sticky notes or a graphic organizer. Or they may do a quick sketch in a margin or on a separate piece of paper to show what they understood. The idea is to help kids interact with the text rather than just reading words.

- Have children read a small part of the text to be sure they experience comprehension. It may just be a page or even a paragraph.

- Have a brief conversation with students about what they've read so far. Look for interest and engagement. Then have them read a bit more and repeat.

- After reading the entire text, have the group discuss what they read. Let them use their sticky notes and books for reference as they share what they learned or understood.

EL TIP: Conversations about reading may take longer with multilingual learners, but don't skip this all-important component of small group reading time. Teach children to self-monitor, reread, and ask for help if they don't understand.

The following chart lists general suggestions for teaching comprehension in small group that improve the learning of *all* students. You will hear echoes of what I suggested for word callers.

LEVELS J–M COMPREHENSION FOCUS TEACHING TIPS

- Break the reading of longer text into sections across several days to deepen comprehension.

- Be sure students know they should read to understand. Encourage them to reread if meaning breaks down.

- Think of your small group time as an opportunity for conversations with readers—before, during, and after reading.

- Observe children when they get a new book. Do they thoughtfully examine the cover and preview the text or just flip to the first page and start reading words?

- Before reading, ask kids about genre and what they expect to see in the text (e.g., *stories have characters, settings, and plots; folktales have threes; informational text may be written in sections with headings telling central ideas*).

- Give kids sticky notes to jot down things related to the lesson focus (e.g., character traits, point of view, text structure).

- Have children use graphic organizers *during* reading, not just as a comprehension check after reading.

- Give students sticky notes to help them interact with the text.

- Teach kids how to take simple notes or draw sketches on the side *during* reading to deepen comprehension, especially when reading about unfamiliar topics.

- Encourage students to reread if they don't comprehend something (a word, a sentence, a section).

Using Sticky Notes and Graphic Organizers

Sticky notes and graphic organizers can help students keep track of what they've read. But not all kids need to use these all the time. Here are a few tips to help you get the most out of using these tools:

- Give kids a specific number of sticky notes to start. For example, if it's nonfiction they're reading, give them three sticky notes and ask them to jot down three things that they learned about the topic, one idea per note.

- Use *simple* graphic organizers for notetaking. Match the task to the organizer. For example, use a story plot map for fiction. Provide a t-chart for two-column notes when students are recording questions and answers while reading.

- Model how to use sticky notes or graphic organizers in whole group before ever expecting kids to do this on their own in small group. Remind students what to do in small group by showing examples of these artifacts from whole group. Ask kids how these notes might help them comprehend to be sure they understand the purpose of doing this kind of reading work.

- Show kids how to place a sticky note in a text with the sticky part near the outer edge of a page (so the note is easy to find and doesn't get lost in the book).

ONLINE LEARNING TIP: Teach students how to use virtual sticky notes and other online highlighting tools while reading. For example, Reading A–Z lets kids stamp stop signs or stars onto the text. They can also jot notes in the margin while reading with a virtual pen.

Introducing Reciprocal Teaching

Reciprocal teaching actively engages students by using four reading strategies: predicting, questioning, clarifying, and summarizing text read. Start by working with each of these strategies in whole group (or possibly small group) before asking students to use all of them in a reciprocal teaching model. Eventually, you will release control and allow students to lead the discussion using these four strategies, with one child owning one strategy. This works best if you break a text into several shorter portions for reading.

Once you're confident that students are familiar with the strategies, make four cards with each naming and picturing one of the strategies. Hand these out to kids in your small group before they read a section of text. Eventually, students may lead these discussions without your assistance.

After reading, each student takes the lead by sharing their thinking using the strategy stated on their card. Others can join in, too. Go around the small group letting each student lead by talking about their strategy. Here are the strategies. Use them in the order that makes sense to you:

1. Question: Ask questions related to the section just read.

2. Clarify: Share words you needed to read more than once to decode or to figure out their meanings. Or tell about parts that were tricky to understand.

3. Summarize: Tell what the text was mostly about in just a few words.

4. Predict: Tell what you think the next section will be about.

Printable reciprocal teaching cards for small group are available in the online companion at **resources.corwin.com/simplysmallgroups**.

 To read more detail about Palincsar and Brown's original work on reciprocal teaching, visit https://bit.ly/3cKDIOo.

 To see a short video about reciprocal teaching with students in the transitional stage of reading, visit https://bit.ly/3f1qVJY.

EL TIP: It's important to teach each of the four steps in reciprocal teaching, one at a time. When students can do one well, add on the next. When they can do all four, they can try reciprocal teaching with less support from the teacher.

Improving Inference

Teachers often lament that their students have difficulty with inference. Inferring is a skill we use in everyday life. We hear the garage door open at 5:30 p.m. and infer that a family member has just come home from work. Or we see a flag blowing outdoors and infer that it is a windy day. Nobody told us these things. We figured them out by using what we already know and the evidence we see or hear. Help students realize that they infer all the time.

Then help them transfer this skill to reading. You can start with having kids make predictions, a simple kind of inference. They might say, "I predict _____ will happen. I think this because I already know _____ . The book also says _____ . So my inference is _____ ."

You might introduce your students to this simple equation in words or pictures:

background knowledge + what the text says = inference

For example, I have played with dominoes and know they can be lined up and tipped over. The text says, "Emily rolled the marble into the first domino," so I infer that the dominoes will push each other over.

Help students think about what they already know. Use ideas from the Build Background Knowledge part of Section 3 on page 128. Then help them connect that to what the book says. Finally, have them tell what they can figure out from that. I often give kids colored sticky notes, as shown in the photo here, to make inferences.

Students use colored sticky notes and an anchor chart to make inferences as they read.

You might also use riddles to help children with inference. Have kids write their own riddles, too.

ONLINE LEARNING TIP: Kids might enjoy playing online games with riddles. Here are a few to try: https://www.riddles.com/quiz/10-easy-riddles, https://www.pocoyo.com/en/riddles, and http://www.philtulga.com/Riddles.html.

Choose Matching Vocabulary Work

Understanding new words can greatly impact comprehension, and at the transitional stage children will encounter words that may not be in their oral language. Therefore, it is important to teach students how to stop and pay attention to new vocabulary while reading.

Vocabulary learning begins with listening and speaking. Children who have heard many new words and assimilated these into their oral language will have better comprehension than those who have limited speaking vocabulary. So read aloud with intention in whole group daily. Choose books with rich vocabulary and think aloud about how to figure out the meanings of new words.

Encourage kids to ask when they don't know what a word means as you read aloud. Children who are curious about new words become children with advanced vocabularies! Be sure to have kids use those new words multiple times to make them stick. For example, *Harm means hurt. Have you ever heard about someone or something being **harmed** or hurt? My house got broken into but nobody was **harmed**.*

EL TIP: Use cognates when working with children who speak Spanish and English. Around 30 percent to 40 percent of all words in English have a related word in Spanish. Here is an excellent cognate list for your reference: https://bit.ly/3tDvJcy.

Children illustrate vocabulary cards to go with a read-aloud or book read in small group.

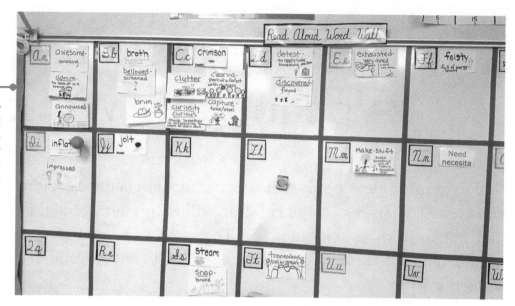

New vocabulary words illustrated by third graders are added to their Word Wall as a visual reminder to use these words while speaking, reading, and writing.

⭐ **EL TIP:** Multilingual learners benefit from retelling. It helps build oral language, comprehension, and vocabulary.

Teach students how to use a dictionary to check on word meaning, too. Keep a dictionary beside you during read-aloud and model how to look up a word kids are unsure about. Think aloud as you search for the word. For example, "*Applicant* starts with the letter *a*, so I will look in the beginning of the dictionary for A words. I scan until I find words that start with the first few letters. Then I slow down. Next, I read the word and its definitions. I think about which meaning matches what I just read. Then I reread the sentence in the book to be sure I understand." Use the same dictionary you want kids to use on their own.

ONLINE LEARNING TIP: Teach students how to use a dictionary or glossary when reading online text, too. Text with hyperlinks that take readers directly to the meaning of that word can be very useful. Here is a sample from Scholastic News, Grade 2 English: https://sn2.scholastic.com.

⭐ **EL TIP:** Online dictionaries are helpful for second-language learners, too.

Here are some teaching tips to consider when helping students at the transitional reading stage develop vocabulary in small group.

LEVELS J–M VOCABULARY FOCUS TEACHING TIPS

- Introduce new vocabulary from the book if there is a word that kids need to comprehend the text well. Model how to use clues from the words and graphics. Have children use this word orally as they talk before reading the book.

- Remind students to pay attention to new words as they read, including figurative language in literary text and bold words in informational text.

- Model how to use a dictionary or glossary during read-aloud. Show how to find word meanings students might just skip over.

- Let kids keep cool little notebooks where they jot down new words.

- Remind students to use new vocabulary as they discuss and summarize what they read.

- Model how to use words and sentences that surround a new word to figure out its meaning.

- Begin to study multiple meaning words, homophones, and idioms at this stage.

Use the photo examples for additional ideas on how to help transitional readers develop new vocabulary. You'll find the matching focus work in bold.

Students are on the lookout for new words as they read. The teacher introduced the word cards, and kids did quick pencil sketches **illustrating word meanings** as they encountered them during small group reading. Word cards are then used to summarize the book after reading or to write responses in follow-up lessons.

What does that word mean?

STOP

?

look

It was a hot sunny day.

think

Use an **anchor chart** like the one pictured to remind readers to stop and pay attention to new words. A matching printable bookmark is included in the online companion at **resources.corwin.com/ simplysmallgroups**. Model with this in whole group and remind kids to do this in small group, too.

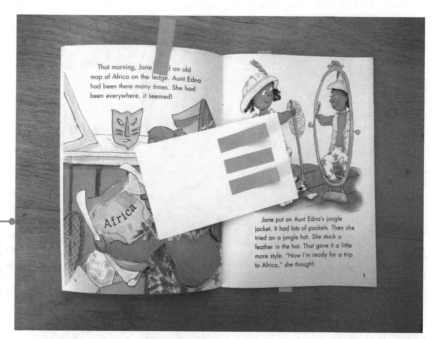

Teach students to **highlight new words** using small pieces of highlighter tape to place over new words they encounter while reading in small group. Or have them put a small sticky note near the word. They use these words while talking about what they read.

ONLINE LEARNING TIP: Children will enjoy WittyWings, where they can swap vocabulary words to change meanings in stories to create their own adventures. It can even be played with two readers. For a preview, go to http://www. wittywings.fr/en.

Kids keep small **vocabulary notebooks** where they jot down new words found. They might add sketches or definitions to go with their new vocabulary. Encourage them to use this notebook during writing, too.

EL TIP: There are so many ways to say something similar in a language! Learning synonyms is a way to extend vocabulary. When learning a new language, students may gather related words but not know the nuanced use until working with the language for many years. For example, the words *grass*, *lawn*, *meadow*, *park*, and *backyard* are connected but don't mean exactly the same thing. It takes kids years to learn which word to use when.

Students place small sticky notes over new vocabulary to do a **synonym swap**. They substitute another word that makes sense in place of the unknown word to figure out its meaning while reading in small group. Then they share these with each other after reading.

Students add to a class **idiom board** during small group reading. As they find an idiom, they write it with thick black marker and add a picture showing its meaning. This increases awareness of figurative language and improves comprehension.

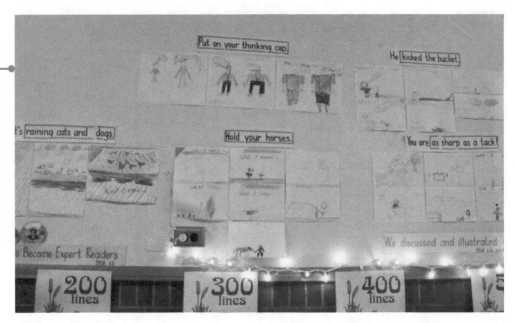

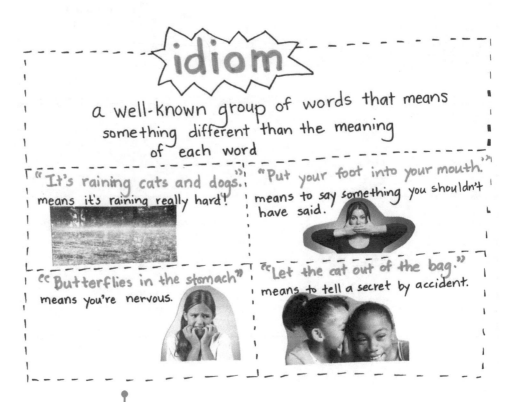

An **idiom anchor chart** made with the class reminds students to be on the lookout for these commonly used expressions as they listen in whole group, read in a small group, or read independently.

An idiom is a commonly used expression. It is a group of words that can't be understood by knowing the literal meaning of its individual words. Here are a few common idioms your children should learn the meanings of:

- As easy as pie
- A piece of cake
- Hit the books
- Up in the air

- Frog in your throat
- Face the music
- Under the weather
- In the same boat

Picture books are wonderful for introducing idioms. Here are a few to try.

- *Raining Cats and Dogs* by Will Moses
- *In a Pickle: And Other Funny Idioms* by Marvin Terban
- *Butterflies in My Stomach and Other School Hazards* by Serge Bloch
- *Amelia Bedelia* series

EL TIP: Idioms can be especially tricky for multilingual learners. Use and explain idioms in everyday conversation to help children learn this nuanced language. Encourage them to ask when they don't understand what words mean.

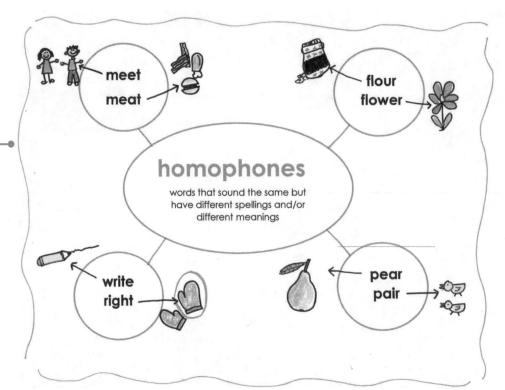

A **homophones anchor chart** is a visual reminder to be on the lookout for words that sound the same but have different spellings and/or different meanings. Kids add to this as they find new words (e.g, *meet*, *meat*).

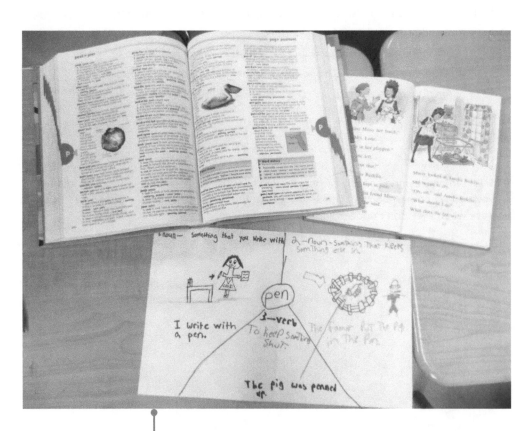

Students make drawings to show the different meanings of a word for a **multiple meaning Word Wall**. Display these on cabinet doors or another wall space as a catalyst for kids to pay attention to this interesting vocabulary variation. You might also make a **homophone wall** beside it.

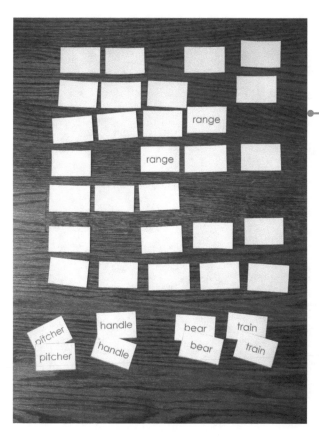

Play a **multiple meaning word memory** game. Each multiple meaning word is written on two cards, which are then placed face down. Take turns flipping over two cards at a time and telling a meaning for each word. If you get a match, you tell a different definition for each word and give an example and keep both cards. The player with the most cards wins.

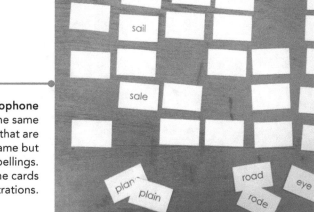

Play a **homophone memory** game in the same way, but use words that are pronounced the same but have different spellings. Kids can make the cards and add simple illustrations.

EL TIP: English learners will benefit from collecting homophones and illustrating them. The more kids play with language, the more they will enjoy learning these nuances.

Students play **Guess My Word** by giving each other clues about vocabulary words. One gives the clues and the other writes the word on a dry erase board to guess. They can act it out, give a definition, or use it in a sentence with a blank. They might use words from science, a Word Wall, or a list they generate from books they've read.

It's important to look at what students *can* do. But sometimes there are clear patterns of where children get stuck along a developmental continuum.

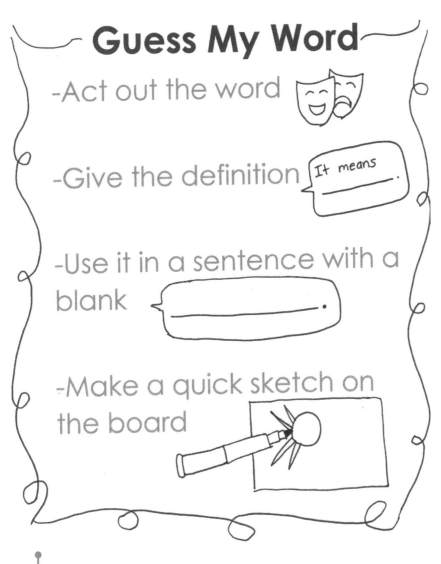

Guess the Word directions for transitional readers can be found in the online companion.

If You See This, Try This . . .

Here are some specific solutions to common sticking points for transitional readers.

IF YOU SEE THIS . . .	TRY THIS:
Try to sound out every letter in a word	• Teach or review blending chunks. Start with the Most Common Phonograms to Use for Decoding printable available on the online companion.
Have trouble with vowel sounds	• Check to be sure the child can identify vowels (*a, e, i, o, u,* and sometimes *y*) and knows the difference between short and long vowels. • Use simple anchor charts with pictures to help kids remember vowel sounds.
Say some of the sounds in a word and make up a word (that may not make sense)	• Say, "You're using some of the sounds and making up a word. Stop doing that. Look at the word. Read the sounds (or parts) in order. Be sure the word makes sense."
Look at you for approval (instead of looking at the words)	• Tell the student to look at the word. Don't make eye contact, but look at the page, too.
Finger point to every word on the page and are reading very choppily	• Suggest that kids use their eyes to read the words instead of finger pointing. There may be too many words or lines on the page. Try a text with less print on the page to move away from finger pointing and improve fluency.
Don't pay attention to punctuation	• Review simple punctuation marks and their purposes. You might have kids use highlighter tape to mark punctuation on a page and practice stopping at these marks.
Read in a monotone voice	• Model how to read a line or two with expression. Then have kids echo read to sound like you. You might teach them how to record their reading of a page so they can listen and hear their expression.

IF YOU SEE THIS . . .	TRY THIS:
Don't read in phrases	• Model how to read in phrases so it sounds like you're talking. Tell kids this will help them understand what they read. • Choose text written in phrases. This will help children train their eyes (and their voice) to move quickly to the end of a phrase. Poems work well for phrased reading, too.
Keep reading even though they don't comprehend	• Set a purpose for reading. • Choose text kids have background knowledge for to aid comprehension. • Have students read just a bit and then discuss what they've read so far. Don't wait until they've read a whole book without comprehending. This develops poor habits.
Decode all (or most) of the words but don't remember what they read	• See suggestions above.
Decode new vocabulary, but don't stop to think about what the word means	• Help students stop and pay attention to new words by giving them cool little notebooks for collecting and illustrating new vocabulary they find as they're reading. • Have students add to specialized Word Walls (e.g., multiple meaning words, homophones, science words). • Play vocabulary games to increase interest in new words and their meanings.

Teaching Fluent Readers

Characteristics *of* Fluent Readers

Students at the *fluent* stage are sometimes also called *independent readers*. They are typically in third or fourth grade and up. These students are becoming more adept at choosing texts that meet their needs and interests. They often read series books to be entertained or to escape. They read informational texts to learn about topics of interest to them or to expand their knowledge. They read online and print versions of a wide variety of text. They may engage in social media.

Students in upper grades may be at the fluent reading stage but still not be reading at grade level. You may have fifth graders reading on a third-grade level. Their comprehension may break down as texts become longer. Or they may not know how to build background knowledge as they read. They may need help understanding new vocabulary. These students are usually aware that they have not progressed on the same trajectory as their peers, so they may lack confidence or feel embarrassed when reading. Reading is difficult for them. Be respectful of these students. Build up their confidence and self-esteem in small groups and work to develop their trust. You can do this by choosing texts that will spark their interest and motivate them to read. Use articles and short stories to build their confidence.

Fluent readers read all kinds of texts. They may read mysteries, fantasy, historical fiction, graphic novels, short stories, poetry, or plays in fiction. Nonfiction genres at this stage include biographies, narrative nonfiction, informational text, and argumentative or persuasive text. Fluent readers often develop preferences for a particular genre. For example, some kids want to only read mysteries while others constantly read informational text about topics of deep interest to them. You might help students explore new genres in small group.

Use guided reading levels (N and up) and corresponding bands of Lexile levels as a guide to choosing text you read with fluent readers. See the information in the online companion on a variety of leveling systems you might use as a reference to grade-level text. (Find the online companion at **resources.corwin .com/simplysmallgroups**.)

At the fluent reading stage, motivation and interest may trump reading levels. Instead of relying solely on guided reading or Lexile levels for book selection, consider what students are curious or passionate about. Help them self-select

EL TIP: Multilingual learners are still developing language at the fluent reading stage. Give them many opportunities to talk with others about what they are reading.

ONLINE LEARNING TIP: Use brief online informational video clips to build background knowledge for new topics. Share videos *before* kids read in small groups and allow students to watch them more than once.

books by authors and about topics they can connect to. For example, if you have kids who love sports and watched a game last night, they might enjoy reading the recap of the event the next day. Even if the text seems at a higher level than students normally read, their background knowledge and interest can drive success. Likewise, children who enjoyed a movie which is also a book can use what they learned from the movie to help them tackle new vocabulary and concepts in the related novel.

Texts are longer for kids at the fluent reading stage. There are subtle changes from one guided reading level to the next. The same holds true for Lexile and other leveling systems. Books and articles have more pages, more print per page, fewer illustrations, and take longer to read. They increase in vocabulary load and text complexity.

Students at this stage can read for longer amounts of time. Fluent readers read silently and can read faster silently than orally. They may get stuck on multisyllable words but are learning to use what they know about vowels and syllable types to decode these words. Likewise, fluent readers are learning to pay attention to unfamiliar words and are extending their vocabulary through reading, especially as they are given opportunities to discuss texts with others.

The fluent reading stage never really ends. Students may need support to build background knowledge, as often they're reading beyond their life experiences. Sentence structure, plots, and content vary in complexity as readers tackle new subjects and genres. Vocabulary demands increase. Understanding of history and cultures affects reading comprehension. As students develop social skills, help them to apply these to online texts and platforms, including social media.

Text samples for fluent reader levels N (left) and T (right).

Fluent Readers *and* Comprehension

Comprehension is at the forefront of the fluent reader stage. We read to create meaning, to make sense of the world, and to learn new things. Fluent readers should be monitoring their comprehension and rereading when meaning breaks down. Review what *comprehension* means, since we often use this word during instruction. If you have students who still need help with monitoring comprehension, see ideas in Section 4 on page 136. Likewise, if you have kids who are just reading words without understanding, see the suggestions in the Solving Word Calling segment on pages 173–174. Although kids at this stage can read many texts independently, they still benefit from hearing stories, poems, and informational text read aloud in whole group. By reading aloud, we can model the love of reading, increase reading motivation, introduce students to new series and genres, and provide opportunities for kids to engage in discussions about text. As you have students turn and talk in response to a read-aloud, they are learning conversational skills to apply in a variety of small groups including book clubs and inquiry groups.

Be sure to engage students in authentic experiences around comprehension. Think about what we do as readers and writers outside of school in the real world to guide your planning. On the next page are a few ideas to try instead of forcing kids to do inauthentic reading and writing tasks.

EL TIP: To build background knowledge, language, and confidence, have multilingual learners watch a video clip and then discuss it in a small group with native speakers. Then students can read a related book and talk about the similarities and differences.

INSTEAD OF MAKING FLUENT READERS DO THIS AT SCHOOL...	TRY THIS:
• Read assigned texts with comprehension questions to "prove" they read	• Invite students to keep a reader's notebook, where they can:
• Write required book reports	○ Write about personal connections they make while reading
• Take an AR test to get points	○ Note new words
• Keep a reading log with the number of pages read and dates	○ Jot natural moments when they pause to think while reading (e.g., a new word encountered, a change in setting, something a character does, confusing information, not sure who is talking in dialogue)
	○ Jot questions that emerged
	A reader's notebook can provide good fodder for student writing, too.
	• Ask kids to share or reflect on their thinking while reading self-selected or assigned texts.
	• Invite readers to do further research to answer any new questions that arose from reading.
	• Model how to write to an author in response to a text read and invite kids to do the same.
	• Provide opportunities for kids to share books they're reading with classmates (e.g., book reviews, book trailers, recommendation wall, classroom book blog or vlog).
	• Compare a book to its movie counterpart—and make an argument for which version is better.
	• Create a Flipgrid presentation about every book finished during a school year or quarter.

Asking Higher-Level Questions

Teach students at the fluent stage how to ask higher-level questions and analyze text. Because students will be required to take state assessments, work with questions that use the language of released items from these tests.

Here are some open-ended, thought-provoking questions kids might use as they discuss what they read, no matter what kind of small group they are in. (There's a printable copy in the online companion to use when planning, too.)

- Compare _____ to _____. How were they the same? How were they different?

- What would have happened if _____?

- What questions would you ask _____ if you could talk to him/her?

- Why do you think _____?

- What is the theme of this story? What makes you think that?

- What is the relationship between _____ and _____?

- Suppose you could _____. What would you do _____?

- Predict what might happen if _____.

- Do you agree with _____? Why or why not?

- What is your opinion of _____?

- Would it be better if _____?

- Why do you think the character did/said/reacted _____?

- Based on what you know, how would you explain _____?

- What would you recommend _____?

Reading With Fluency

Fluency affects comprehension, too. Students at the fluent reading stage will need to apply what they knew about fluent reading of shorter text to longer pieces. They should continue to read in phrases and to read with expression silently (as well as when sharing a text aloud in small group discussions). If you have students in the fluent reading stage who need some help with fluency, see pages 163–170 in Section 4.

High-frequency word work is typically not needed at this stage since most words kids read are now sight words—words they can read quickly and easily because they've read them previously many times.

EL TIP: Provide higher-level thinking sentence stems to support multilingual students' development of academic language, beyond basic conversational English.

Choosing Books

Examine students' book choices as you plan to help their comprehension deepen. As you work with fluent readers, observe them reading independently. Think about the following to plan the next steps for small group:

- How do your fluent readers choose books?

- What kinds of text do they read?

- Are they reading mostly one genre? Which? Why?

- Do they usually finish books or have a habit of abandoning them?

- What do they typically do before reading?

- How do they respond to what they've read?

Choosing text is important for all students at this stage but especially those who don't read much. Allow students to choose short informational articles rather than novels. Some may choose to read on devices rather than print copies. Get to know your kids and build on their interests and preferences. The key is to get them reading and build their volume of positive reading experiences.

Talking About Books

Listen to fluent readers talking about books, too. Which of the following do they do?

- Share details from texts read

- Listen to others and build on those ideas

- Talk about their connections and personal experiences related to the text

- Recommend other books to their peers

- Use expanding vocabulary, sometimes referring to new words from the text

- Demonstrate a positive (or negative) attitude toward reading

EL TIP: Listen to multilingual learners talk about what they are reading to other students. Do they share with other students who speak their home language? Are they comfortable talking about books with native speakers?

Fluent Readers *and* Vocabulary

Vocabulary load continues to increase at fluent levels, so continue to teach students to be on the lookout for new words. Learning Greek and Latin roots can help kids determine meanings of some new words. Encourage students to keep a small vocabulary notebook to jot down new words (and meanings) encountered as they read. Vocabulary affects comprehension, especially at this stage where there is little to no support in pictures in fiction and more content vocabulary in informational text.

Multilingual and dyslexic learners especially benefit from **morphological awareness**. A **morpheme** is the smallest unit of meaning in a word. Learning about affixes and roots helps students identify and understand difficult academic vocabulary that increases in texts at the fluent reading stage.

EL TIP: On average it takes students learning English as a new language three to five years to develop oral proficiency and four to seven years to develop academic proficiency. Help them acquire the academic vocabulary needed so they can participate in social and more academic discussions.

Paying Attention to New Words

As fluent readers encounter new words, they may still stumble over decoding and pronunciation. Review how to decode long words (see page 162 in Section 4 for ideas) and how to use a pronunciation key online or in a print dictionary. Model by using a device with a dictionary app when reading aloud to students. Or use a print dictionary some days. Show students how to easily look up a word they're unsure of and hear how to pronounce it.

Many kids will just skip over words they don't understand and keep going. Model how to slow down and work through a word by stopping and thinking about the meaning of the word. For example, in the sentence *"He was undeniably the best candidate for the job,"* instead of moving past the words *undeniably* or *candidate*, stop and think about another word you could use that would still make sense there; try *"He was certainly the best person for the job."* Show kids how to search around the word for clues to its meaning, as well as how to use a dictionary to find out the word's meaning.

You might have kids keep a small notebook where they jot down new words to help them think about discovering new vocabulary. They could put a letter at the top of each page, from A to Z, and jot the new word down on the page matching its first letter. Or they may make a page with a book title at the top and the new words found in that book. The key is to find a way to organize words that will help students use them.

Invite children to share their new words with each other in small groups. Encourage them to use their new vocabulary while writing, too. The more they use these words, the more likely they will increase their vocabulary.

Fluent reader's vocabulary journal.

Learning Greek and Latin Roots

Morphological awareness is the key to unlocking word meaning. Help fluent readers understand the importance of learning Greek and Latin roots as they explore the English language at higher reading levels. You might share these facts with your students to pique their interest:

- More than 90 percent of academic words in English come from Latin and Greek roots. Many of these words are used in science.

- Knowing one Greek or Latin root can help you understand ten or more words in English.

- You can figure out the meanings of words you've never seen or heard before just by using your knowledge of Greek or Latin roots. For example, if you know that *multi* means *many*, you can figure out the meaning of *multidimensional*: having many dimensions.

Have kids be on the lookout for words with Greek and Latin roots. Start with roots that are used most frequently in the texts students are reading. Also review affixes (prefixes and suffixes) from previous grades. (See page 161 in

Section 4.) I recommend making clear, simple lists with your class. This is fun to do in the form of a tree, as shown in the photo.

For a useful list of Greek and Latin roots, check out this article from Reading Rockets: https://bit.ly/3oYpc9t.

EL TIP: Here is a useful list of twenty-five Lat in roots and their connection to cognates in Spanish and English: https://bit.ly/3qzVSai.

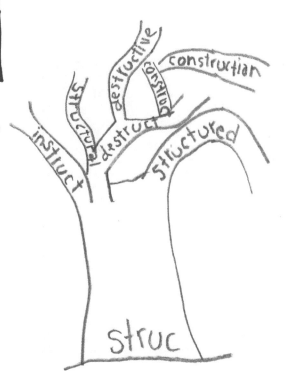

Greek and Latin root charts made with fourth graders. Kids can add on words they find in their books with small sticky notes.

Greek and Latin root trees made by kids show the interconnectedness between words.

ONLINE LEARNING TIP: The visual root trees at https://membean.com/treelist can help students see the connections between words. Kids can make their own Greek and Latin word trees with words they find in their reading.

Start *by* Looking *at* What Students *Can* Do *and* Want *to* Learn About

Now that we've looked at the importance of comprehension and vocabulary for fluent readers, let's examine what to do in small group instruction. By the time students reach the fluent stage, some are voracious readers with clearly defined interests who always have books on deck for their next read. Others have struggled on the way to the fluent reader stage, taking much longer than their peers to get here. Some students *can* read but choose not to. Still others read words without understanding at times. Look at what students *can* do and also what they are *interested in* as you think about small groups.

The chart below can guide you in planning small group instruction based on what you see children are able to do. Use these strengths to help kids grow as independent fluent readers.

Fluent Readers May Be Able to . . .

LEVELS N AND UP	HELP THEM GROW WITH WHAT THEY KNOW
Have well-defined interests	Help kids find books that match their interests and other kids who like to read about the things they do. Build a community of readers.
Have favorite series or authors	Expand kids' knowledge of series and authors to find new texts to read. Help them learn from these authors to improve their own writing, too.
Understand how stories work	Help students expand their understanding of story structure as they learn about flashbacks and foreshadowing. Also encourage them to read new genres.

LEVELS N AND UP	HELP THEM GROW WITH WHAT THEY KNOW
• Recognize and use text features in informational text	• Remind students to read one section at a time in informational text. They should continue to read *all* the information, including text features. Remind them to summarize each section as read.
• Infer when reading text they have background knowledge for	• Model how to use what kids know *plus* what the text says when reading longer or less familiar text.
• Easily decode multisyllable words	• Help kids use Greek and Latin roots to understand what new words mean. Also teach them about pronunciation keys.
• Reread to fix up words and keep meaning going	• Encourage children to self-monitor and be sure they are understanding, especially on longer texts. Help them understand it's still okay to reread.
• Decode words but not know their meanings	• Use word hunts to find words with prefixes, suffixes, and Greek and Latin roots to build word meanings. • Help kids be "word builders" and "word collectors."
• Spell most one-syllable words correctly • Confuse spellings in multisyllable words, especially at the syllable juncture (unsure about when to double consonants, drop *e*) • Use but confuse long vowel patterns, especially when writing words with more than one syllable	• Teach students syllable patterns to help their reading and writing. • Use word hunts to find words with spelling patterns students are using but confusing.
• Write stories or informational texts	• Help students develop their voice and craft as writers by using the books they read as models. • Learn to publish and write for authentic purposes.

Plan *and* Teach Lessons That Match *the* Needs *of* Your Students

As you work with students at fluent reading levels in small group, realize that they are still growing as readers. They are learning to use reading for a variety of purposes throughout their lives, both in and out of school. The more kids read and the more exposure they have to a wide variety of texts, combined with instruction in small groups, the more they can learn. For example, reading historical fiction set during the American Revolution can help students understand what they're learning about in social studies. Likewise, reading fantasy can help prepare them for solving problems in real life.

EL TIP: Silent letters and suffixes, such as *tion*, *sion*, and *cian* are challenging for native speakers and multilingual learners. Doing word hunts and word sorts with these morphemes can help with decoding, vocabulary, and comprehension.

Although the focus at this stage will be on comprehension and vocabulary, continue to pay attention to how kids decode multisyllable words. They may still need to review and work with syllable types when figuring out new words. You may include a bit of advanced phonics work (e.g., *tion*, *sion*, *able*, *ible*) in isolation in small groups, but always move that decoding into connected text so that students learn to apply those skills. Review syllable types as needed, too. (See pages 153–154 in Section 4 for ideas.)

Keep meaning at the forefront and include comprehension and vocabulary as part of each lesson. Use small group time to help fluent readers become strategic meaning-makers.

MATERIALS NEEDED for SMALL GROUPS at this STAGE

- Fiction and informational texts at Levels N and above
- Series books
- Short stories, reader's theater or plays, and poems
- Informational texts and articles
- Argumentative texts

- Procedural texts

- Biographies

- Dictionaries and thesauruses

- Text sets about topics of interest

- Anchor charts with syllable patterns

- Simple graphic organizers for comprehension

- Sticky notes and pencils

- Highlighter tape

- Vocabulary notebooks

- Small whiteboard and plate stand for a Focus Board

- Contacts with local organizations for students to communicate with

MATERIALS NEEDED for ONLINE SMALL GROUPS

- Paper and markers (for writing)

- Virtual vocabulary walls (use a Google Slide with a 5-x-5 table inserted)

- Digital texts

- Drive-through family pickup of materials, including books, paper, dictionaries, thesauruses, whiteboards and dry erase supplies, vocabulary notebooks, highlighter tape, simple graphic organizers, and sticky notes

EL TIP: Children learning a second language benefit from listening to text read aloud to hear pronunciations and language inflections. Let them use text-to-speech assisted technology or listen to audio books.

What *to* Look *for in* Text *for* Fluent Readers

As students move into higher reading levels, text choice is important to their growth both in small group and independent reading time. Don't restrict kids only to "books on their level." You might use guided reading levels (as well as Lexile levels at the fluent stage) to gauge student growth—but these are intended as assessment and instructional tools, not as identifiers. Be careful not to pigeon-hole kids into these levels. Sometimes it's fun to read something a bit easier, and this can keep fluency intact as well as lengthen the time children spend reading.

Observe students and help them follow their interests. Stay abreast of children's literature so you can make book recommendations. Provide graphic novels, informational text, and hi-lo books like those from Saddleback Books for students in the fluent reading stage who are not reading at grade level. Encourage kids to recommend books to each other, too.

Students in Grades 3 and up are required to take standardized reading tests in most schools. Therefore, you will want them to be familiar with how to take tests. But be sure that you do more than assign passages with comprehension questions. Provide daily opportunities for fluent readers to engage in reading texts they choose to read independently, in small groups, or with a partner.

Ask yourself these questions when looking for text for kids in the fluent reader stage:

- Are you exposing fluent readers to an ever-widening selection of genres? Are students choosing to read new and varied kinds of texts?

- Does this text address issues and interests relevant to your students?

- Will this book or article encourage kids to read related texts?

- Is this book part of a series? Will it help students recognize themes across texts?

- Does this book connect to historical or cultural events that will expand the students' worldview? Is it historically accurate and culturally representative?

- Does this text match what your students need to practice (e.g., analyzing plot elements including rising action, climax, falling action, and resolution; understanding shifts in time with flashback or foreshadowing; identifying the claim and how the author has used facts to support an argument)?

- Does this book have a strong voice? Can your students examine it from the perspective of a writer as well as a reader?

- Are kids reading books by a wide variety of authors? Are those authors from diverse backgrounds with authentic voices?

- Are your students reading full books and articles instead of just passages?

- Are you giving your children opportunities to read a mix of digital and print texts?

- Are students reading as much nonfiction as fiction? Or more?

- Are you providing opportunities for students who don't read at grade level to listen to books and articles written at higher levels to help them access more complex text?

EL TIP: Are your multilingual students reading (and writing) in more than one language?

A Variety *of* Small Group Options *for* Fluent Readers

Although most students at this stage are reading independently, fluent readers can still benefit from working in small groups. Depending on their needs, choose from the type of small group that will best benefit the child. Vary who is in small groups throughout the year based on student interest and progress. Also think about how often each group will meet. You might meet with a guided reading group two or three times a week. A book club might meet once or twice a week. And a writing group might meet every other week. Here is a chart summarizing several small group options for fluent readers.

The remainder of this section describes each type of small group for fluent readers and includes sample lesson plans and ideas of what to focus on in each kind of small group. Remember that students may be in different types of small groups during the year. During one week you may meet with one group for guided reading, a different group for writing, and still another group who are doing inquiry. Students may be in more than one group at a time. For example, Jake may be in an inquiry group studying video game creation that meets on Tuesday and in a Thursday writing group focused on composing graphic novels. Be flexible. There is no one right way to work with small groups at the fluent reader stage. Follow the lead (and interests) of your students.

EL TIP: Be sure that students acquiring a new language have opportunities to meet in small groups with children who are native speakers.

TYPE OF GROUP	HOW OFTEN TO MEET	WHO NEEDS THIS?	BENEFITS OF THIS TYPE OF GROUP	TYPES OF TEXT TO USE
Guided reading group	• Might meet three to four times a week for several weeks • Teacher-led group	• Students with surface or limited comprehension • Readers who have difficulty decoding multisyllable words • Students learning to read a new genre • Kids who skip over words they don't know	• Specific instruction and support focused on student need • Can be temporary groups, based on need • Can use data to form these groups	• Leveled books and articles • Short stories • Poems • Reader's theater/dramas
Book club	• Meet weekly for discussion • Read book independently many days in preparation for discussion • Teacher meets with the group to start but then can be student-led	• Students who have a favorite author or genre • Readers who may need motivation and would be encouraged by peer discussion • Kids who comprehend but could go deeper	• Deeper comprehension • Oral language development • Social interaction as kids talk about books • Establishes a community of readers	• Chapter books • Novels • Graphic novels • May be genre-specific (e.g., mystery book club, dog lover book club)

(Continued)

(*Continued*)

TYPE OF GROUP	HOW OFTEN TO MEET	WHO NEEDS THIS?	BENEFITS OF THIS TYPE OF GROUP	TYPES OF TEXT TO USE
Inquiry group	• May meet two to four times a week • Do some independent or partner research in preparation for meetings • Teacher-led to start but released to kids over time	• Children with passionate interests • Students who need motivation to read • Kids who need a nudge toward reading informational text	• Deep exploration of a variety of topics • Can use interest to form these groups • Establishes a community of inquirers • Builds academic vocabulary	• Informational texts around topics of interest • Interviews of experts • Articles and reputable online sources
Writing group	• Meet one to three times a week • Teacher-led	• Students who want to (or need to) improve some aspect of their writing	• Peers can provide support for others as writers • Can help kids get ideas of what to write about and how to strengthen their writing	• Model texts representing the types of writing kids are working on • Pieces kids have written

[Guided Reading Groups]

Some students will grow as readers by being in guided reading groups at Levels N and up. For example, if you have readers who are having difficulty with decoding multisyllable words, help them with this skill in guided reading. Likewise, if you have kids who need support with inference or determining theme, help to guide their thinking in a guided reading group.

Most guided reading sessions for fluent readers will last about twenty to twenty-five minutes. As you choose a focus for each lesson, think about what you want to see kids do independently when they read. Use the Key Reading Behaviors for Fluent Levels chart in the online companion as a guide.

Meet with students in guided reading on a temporary basis until you see those focus reading behaviors in place. Then students may move into a book club or an inquiry group to keep them growing as readers.

The chart below provides an outline for working with students at the fluent reading stage. A guided reading lesson plan template is available in the online companion, **resources.corwin.com/simplysmallgroups**.

GUIDED READING AT THE FLUENT READING STAGE (LEVELS N AND UP)	
Reading behavior to focus on (two to three minutes)	• Use a reading Focus Board. Model what you expect kids to do as readers today. The focus might relate to comprehension, fluency, or vocabulary, depending on their needs. Use the Key Reading Behaviors for Fluent Levels (in the online companion) for ideas. Stick with the focus for several lessons.
Before reading (two to three minutes)	• Ask kids what they do first. Be sure they read the title, scan the book and table of contents, identify the genre and accompanying characteristics, and *think* before reading. Have them tell what they will read to find out. Provide support as needed. • Decide how far kids will read (a chapter, a section, several pages) before stopping to discuss the text. You might have them put a sticky note in the book to show where they will stop. • If students are reading a text over several days, have them reread a bit and summarize what they've read so far. They should preview the next part and set a purpose for reading.

(Continued)

(Continued)

GUIDED READING AT THE FLUENT READING STAGE (LEVELS N AND UP)	
During reading (seven to ten minutes)	• Students at this stage should read silently. Listen to individuals whisper read a bit to you while the others read on their own. Have a brief conversation with each student after you listen to them read to check for comprehension. • Give kids sticky notes or a simple graphic organizer to jot something you want them to pay attention to (e.g., character traits, problem, a new fact).
After reading (four to five minutes)	• Discuss what kids read. Start with what they read to find out. • Ask one or two higher-level questions. Use the language of released state tests if you have access to these. • Have students share what they tried related to the reading behavior focus (e.g., find a word with the phonics pattern, read a bit of dialogue with expression, show a new word they learned and tell what it means). • Remind kids to keep using that reading focus as they read throughout the day.
In the next lesson . . .	• If the book is long and kids only read part of it, review what they read the day before. Then have them repeat the lesson steps as they read the next part of the book. Stick with the same reading behavior focus if that is what readers need. • If they finished the book, you might do a small group writing lesson the next time these kids meet.

EL TIP: Take extra time with vocabulary. Provide support for multilingual students to use new words as they talk about the text. Ask higher-level questions to help them engage in using academic language.

Focus on Key Reading Behaviors in Guided Reading Groups

Time is limited in small groups, so choose a focus that will propel your students forward as readers. Work with one or two of these reading behaviors at a time in a guided reading group.

Use a Focus Board for each lesson to help students know what to pay attention to. Examples follow. You might use the same focus for multiple lessons (until you see children using that strategy or skill consistently).

In the blank small group reading lesson plan template included, you'll see a space for a *reading behavior to focus on*. If a small group needs help decoding long words, make that the lesson focus. If kids need to work on identifying theme, that will be the focus.

Remember to include comprehension in every guided reading lesson! This often includes vocabulary, especially with informational text. See the list of Key Reading Behaviors for Fluent Levels (Levels N and Up) found as a printable in the online companion, **resources.corwin.com/ simplysmallgroups**.

I recommend giving fluent readers sticky notes to jot something specific as they read. If the focus is on paying attention to character traits, have them write a few words on a sticky note about that character. Or if you want them to infer, have them jot their inference on the sticky note where they made it. This will make it easier for kids to interact with text and provide help for discussions related to comprehension. They might also jot down new vocabulary words as they read and discuss these after reading.

ONLINE LEARNING TIP: If students don't have sticky notes at home, they can jot notes on a piece of paper or in a notebook. Virtual sticky notes are included if you use Reading A–Z.

Not every fluent reader needs to be in a guided reading group. Use guided reading to help kids extract deeper meaning from text, explore flashback or other literary devices, investigate argumentative text, learn new vocabulary, or try a new genre with teacher support.

EL TIP: Have multilingual students simply jot a question mark beside words or parts they didn't understand. Then use these to guide the discussion of what they read.

Book Clubs

For fluent readers who don't need as much teacher support, book clubs are another small group option. Book clubs—small groups where kids read and discuss texts they choose—can deepen comprehension, give new perspectives, and create community. Kids may even read books they wouldn't normally finish by themselves.

Students who aren't reading at grade level may be motivated by being part of a book club with higher-level texts. If they sign up for a book that's more difficult than they can read independently, provide audiobook options or speech-to-text assisted technology.

Sometimes book clubs are also called literature discussion groups or literature circles. I've even called guided reading groups "book clubs" so all kids feel like they are a part of reading and talking about books. (NOTE: Just remember that guided reading groups have more teacher support than the book clubs I'm describing here.) Students might read books or articles in these clubs.

The chart below shows how book clubs usually operate, with accompanying teacher roles.

HOW BOOK CLUBS WORK	TEACHER ROLE
1. Form a group.	Use a sign-up sheet with limited numbers of spaces for each book (or article) title.
2. Choose what to read.	Building on student interests and reading levels, provide three or four choices, and let kids decide which book (or article) they want to read.
3. Decide how far to read and when to meet next.	Coordinate this by having a calendar posted for the class to see.
4. Read on your own and prepare for discussion.	Provide independent reading time and remind book club kids to read those texts.

HOW BOOK CLUBS WORK	TEACHER ROLE
5. Meet in book club and talk about what you read.	Be part of this group to start. Model and teach kids how to talk about books (or articles).
6. Decide how far to read and when the next meeting will be.	Guide the group in the beginning. Students might meet once or twice a week.
7. Repeat steps 4–6.	Be part of the group as long as needed. Then just drop in to visit and listen to students' discussion.

Join as the facilitator of a student book club to start. Read what your kids are reading. Prepare for discussion, just as you expect them to. During book club meetings, model and guide how to talk about texts and include everyone in the discussion. Schedule book club meetings for about twenty minutes or so to keep kids interested and engaged.

When choosing texts for book clubs, here are a few tips:

- Choose books that have something to talk about—conflict, characters that grow or change, or topics and themes that are meaningful to your students (e.g., friendship, telling the truth, loss, being different).

- You might center a book club around a genre. For example, provide choices that are all mysteries or are all historical fiction set during a particular time.

- Try a poetry club where students read poems by a certain poet or around a topic or theme.

- Use nonfiction books or articles, too. You might choose informational articles around a topic of study related to science or social studies to increase background knowledge.

- Start with shorter texts clearly divided into chapters or sections. This may make it easier for kids to finish reading assignments on time for book club discussions.

EL TIP: Multilingual learners may join book clubs with texts at a higher level if you provide an option for them to hear the text read, such as audiobooks and speech-to-text enabled options.

Preparing for Discussion in Book Clubs

To help kids prepare for discussion, give them open-ended questions to reflect on or things to think about as they read. You'll find printable Book Club Questions in the online companion for fiction, nonfiction, and poetry. Here are several ways to use these questions:

- Give each book club member the same question(s) to answer while reading.

- Give each book club member a different question to answer while reading.

- Give two students in the book club the same question(s) to answer while reading.

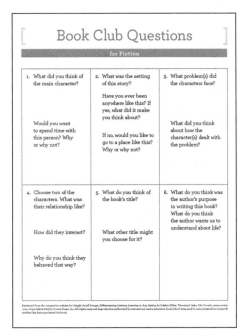

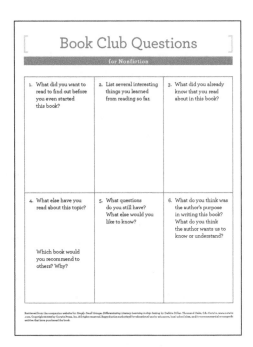

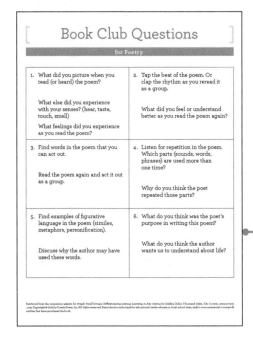

Printable copies of these Book Club Questions are available at **resources .corwin.com/ simplysmallgroups.**

Another option is to have kids use sticky notes as they read. Students might even put a punctuation mark or emoji on the note to match the following:

- A sentence or paragraph that really made you stop and think (stop sign emoji)

- A place where you had a question (question mark)

- A spot where a question you had was answered (period)

- A part that made you laugh (smiley face emoji)

- A place that made you cry (crying emoji)

- Something that surprised you (surprised emoji face)

You might meet with one book club several times to help participants establish routines. Then invite a new group to learn from them in a fishbowl fashion. Have your established book club group sit in the middle with the other kids seated around them in a circle to observe. Invite the "viewers" to jot down what they see kids doing in the book club, paying attention to specific behaviors and routines. After the book club meets, have the "viewers" share their observations and ask questions to learn how to run their own book club.

If you'd like to view a video of fourth graders discussing *The Year of the Boar and Jackie Robinson* in a book club, visit this link: https://bit.ly/3t8fTGB. You might want to show it to kids, too, as an example of a rich book club discussion.

Supporting Book Clubs With Guided Reading Groups

You can meet with kids in a guided reading group to support them as they begin to read a new book. After they understand the characters and plot, switch the structure to a book club where students read with others with less support from you. You can still dip into the group meeting to listen to their discussion and guide as needed. The chart that follows offers a structure for a small group meeting for book clubs.

When kids work together in book clubs, they will probably read several chapters before each meeting. They won't meet daily but should read every day to meet their reading goals and prepare for the next book club meeting. Help kids establish these goals when they meet for the first few times. Eventually, students can set their own goals. Post a sample meeting format like the one that follows to help students stay on track. One student may be the timekeeper for the group.

ONLINE LEARNING TIP: Online learners can meet in book clubs, too. Post a description of each text choice for the book clubs. You might make a short book trailer for each book. Use a Google Doc or Padlet for students to sign up for what they'd like to read.

ONLINE LEARNING TIP: Fluent readers might work in breakout rooms for book clubs, inquiry groups, or writing groups. Create a list of expectations and shared responsibilities for these groups. Occasionally drop into the groups once they are established. You can record breakout rooms and watch them later, too.

SMALL GROUP MEETING FOR BOOK CLUBS

Opening (three minutes)	Check in with members: • Does everyone have their book? • Did everyone finish the reading? • Is everyone prepared for discussion? • What did you think of the book so far?
Book discussion (ten to fifteen minutes)	Have kids take turns being the leader of the group. • Everyone should participate in the discussion. • Take turns talking about answers to questions used while reading. • Take turns sharing sticky notes and making comments.
Closing (three minutes)	• Summarize what the group discussed. • Decide how far to read until the next meeting. • Plan for when the group meets again. • Assign what members should take notes on/think about until next time.

Before starting book clubs, there are many things to teach your students. Model these in whole group during read-aloud. Have kids practice in pairs, then in groups of three or even four students. In whole group, teach and provide opportunities for students to

- Talk about books

- Take notes/find interesting things to share in their discussions

- Take turns while talking in a small group

- Invite others in the group into the discussion

- Agree or disagree with another's point of view

- Ask for clarification if they don't understand something

In addition, teach kids to do these things while you support them when the book club is in session:

- Set a reading goal of how many pages to read daily (to finish reading for the book club meeting on time)

- Be a discussion group leader

- Be a timekeeper

What About Role Cards?

You may notice that I *did not* include role cards or sheets in my suggestions for book clubs. Although role cards are meant to be a support, they often become a crutch for kids and actually stifle the discussion.

Much richer, more natural discussion emerges when we give kids a few questions or sticky notes like those suggested on pages 216–217 to prepare for discussion. Instead of having students be a Word Wizard or an Artful Artist, let students share what they thought or learned from their reading.

I do recommend having someone be the discussion leader, usually a student with the ability to focus the discussion. This person can help start the conversation and be sure everyone participates. They can keep the talk going and move to a new question as needed. Likewise, a timekeeper can keep the group on track to meet their goals.

You might rotate the role of discussion leader, but be sure it is someone who can lead the group. For example, you might start off as the discussion leader to model what this role looks like. Once a student shows leadership in the group, transfer the role to that child. One student might be the discussion leader for multiple sessions, or a different student might lead the conversation for each meeting. You can find printable discussion leader and timekeeper signs in the online companion that can be placed in front of the student with that role as a reminder.

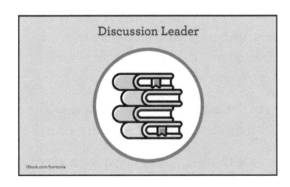

Discussion Leader

iStock.com/bortonia

Timekeeper

Devooda/Shutterstock.com

ONLINE LEARNING TIP: Teach students to rename their "square" in your online classroom platform as Discussion Leader or Timekeeper during book club meetings. Be sure the timekeeper has a copy of the suggested schedule and all members have a copy of the group's goals.

Exploring Themes and Author's Purpose Through Book Clubs

Exploring themes, or messages told through stories, provides opportunities for rich discussion in book clubs. Be sure not to confuse *topic* with *theme*, though. *Theme* is what the author wants us to understand about life; it's a universal, relatable truth that goes beyond what happens to characters in a story. Themes are connected to topics in a story. *Topics* are usually just one word (e.g., *family*, *friendship*, *courage*). *Themes* are what the author wants us to understand about that topic (e.g., *having a friend can help us be brave*).

You might want to organize a book club around a theme. Choose several books with a similar message. This will give students the opportunity to make connections between books and explore the variety of ways different authors approached a theme. You might challenge kids to find other books that relate to that theme, too. Picture books work well for this. A good resource for related books with strong themes is https://socialjusticebooks.org. Look under Reviews and scroll down for related titles.

The author's purpose and theme are intertwined. Examining *why* an author wrote a piece may be connected to events or personal experiences in the author's life that inspired the story. The author's purpose is so much more than PIE (persuade, inform, entertain).

EL TIP: Multilingual learners will love finding and sharing information about authors who spoke another language before learning English.

I love finding video clips or interviews of an author to share with students as they read a book by that writer. Often the authors tell about their inspiration for writing a piece. Voila! Author's purpose and theme described in one easy step. Plus kids see that authors are real people with authentic lives. Everyone has a story to tell. Here is a link to go with the picture book *Love* by Matt de la Peña, to get you started: https://n.pr/2MLet5m.

Eventually, students might try to find author interviews and videos to share with the group to accompany books they are reading or want to read in book club.

Here are a few things to have kids think about as they prepare for book club discussions around theme and author's purpose:

- Choose an important character from the book. What are you learning about this character? How did the illustrator depict this character?

- What do you think the author is trying to teach us about life through this character?

- What do you think the author's purpose is for writing this book?

- What is the theme of this book?

- Connect the theme of this book to your life.

- How does the theme of this book connect to another book? How were the characters similar? Different?

- Do you think the author speaks a language other than English? How did the author use his or her experience of learning English in writing this text?

Examining Point of View in Book Clubs

Point of view is important for students to understand as they develop deeper comprehension as readers and voice as writers. Book clubs can be used to help kids delve into point of view.

To start, be sure students understand what point of view is. Point of view can be simply defined as "who is telling a story" in fiction. Make an anchor chart with your students to help them remember point of view. See the example in the photo below. Kids may enjoy learning and using this rap about point of view on the Flocabulary website: https://bit.ly/2YY2SCE.

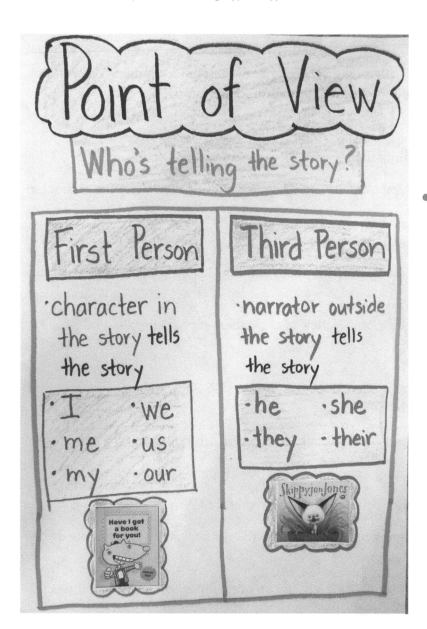

Anchor chart on point of view in fiction.

Guide students to think about who is talking at various points in a story. Help them examine the story from different points of view, including a main character, a different character, or the narrator. Discuss what that person's point of view is and how they know. And talk about how altering the point of view might change a story.

Fractured fairy tales make good choices for book clubs around point of view. Kids love The Other Side of the Story series with titles such as *For Sure, I Paraded in My Underpants!: The Story of the Emperor's New Clothes as Told by the Emperor*, and *Listen, My Bridge Is So Cool: The Story of the Three Billy Goats Gruff as Told by the Troll*. Have them read the original version and compare it to the fractured tale, keeping a focus on how a different point of view changes our understanding of the story.

Nonfiction also offers opportunities for examining point of view. Talk about who is narrating and what their position is. This works for informational and argumentative text. Also have kids share their own point of view about what they read.

Here are a few questions specific to point of view to help students incorporate this aspect of comprehension into their book discussions:

For fiction . . .

- Who is telling the story?

- Is there a narrator? What does the narrator know that the characters don't?

- What is the point of view of _____? (character or narrator)

- How did (or would) the story change if told from a different point of view?

- Compare the point of view of two different characters.

For nonfiction . . .

- What point of view does the writer take? Show evidence of this point of view.

- If there was a debate about this topic, which side would the author take?

- What is your point of view about this topic?

- Do you agree or disagree with the author? Why?

- What experiences do you think the author had that influenced their point of view?

- What other point of view might be possible when considering this topic?

Looking at Genre Characteristics in Book Clubs

It's important for students to understand and use the characteristics of genre when reading. For example, historical fiction has characters and settings that reflect a particular time in history, with fictional characters that are appropriate for that time. So, if I'm reading a story set during the Great Depression, I expect the characters to be trying hard to make ends meet. The plot of the story may revolve around overcoming adversity. It's helpful if I know something about that time period, but I can pay close attention to the text to learn about that time period.

Likewise, if I'm reading fantasy, I expect a story that has magical or supernatural elements as well as a clear beginning, middle, and end. If I'm reading a biography, I expect important details told sequentially about a real person's life and accomplishments.

Help kids in book clubs tap into using what they know (or are learning) about genre as they read and discuss. You might construct or use genre anchor charts with the book club to aid in discussion.

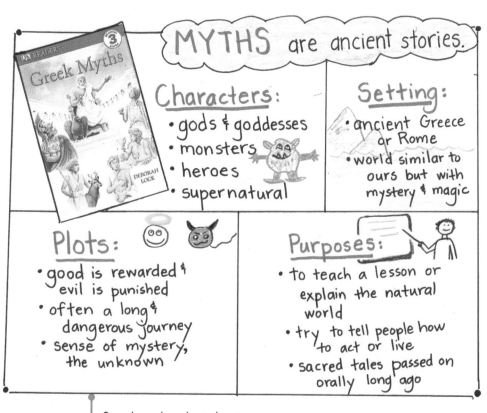

Sample anchor chart about genre characteristics includes photos of books from that genre.

Here a few genre-specific questions kids might answer to prepare for book club discussions:

- What is this book's genre? How do you know?

- What are some characteristics of this genre?

- How did knowing the genre help you understand what you read?

- How might this text change if it was written in a different genre?

Enjoy participating in book clubs with your fluent readers. Follow their lead for ideas of what they'd like to read and talk about. But don't be afraid to use book clubs to help students develop deeper reading skills, as described above, too. For more ideas and lessons on using book clubs, see my book, *Simply Stations: Independent Reading*, pages 121–135. The pictures that follow are a few of the anchor charts included in that book that may help you get started with book clubs in small group.

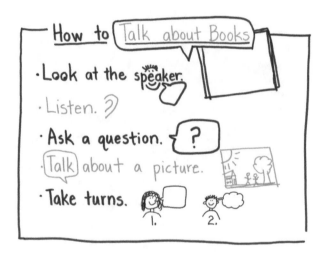

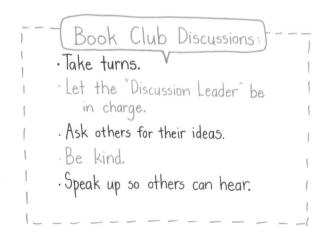

Sample anchor charts for Book Club.

Inquiry Groups

A third type of small group for fluent readers is an inquiry group. This kind of group may motivate students who don't really like to read or who don't choose stories as their go-to genre. The key is to find out what kids are interested in and then help them find text that fires them up to read for information. As you get to know your class, pay attention to topics kids are interested in—ballet, rap, sharks, art, basketball, social justice, video games. Form small inquiry groups based on student interest.

For example, you might have several students who are passionate about recycling. They might meet to read about and discuss recycling, identify a related cause or problem to solve in the community, and then present and enact an action plan to bring about improvement. Or you might have kids who are interested in a sports team who read about recent games and learn more about certain athletes. They may even write to an athlete for further information.

These groups will probably meet a few times a week. Schedule meetings for about twenty minutes to keep engagement strong, and assign a student role of timekeeper to keep things on track.

Create a Climate of Curiosity

Start by encouraging students to ask questions. You might create a Wonder Wall using a bulletin board where kids can post their questions. If you place it near the classroom library, kids will have easy access to books to explore for answers. Model your own curiosity to set the stage. Tell kids what you wonder about and post your questions, too. For example, recently I was paying attention to winter clouds and wondered about how the clouds are different in cold weather and hot weather; my inquiry questions might be "How do clouds change in cold weather? What types of clouds are more common when it's cold?" As I wrote this book, my house had water damage which prompted questions such as "What is ice damming? What causes it? How do you prevent it?"

ONLINE LEARNING TIP: You might create an online Wonder Wall using an app like Padlet. Kids type their questions on virtual sticky notes and post them.

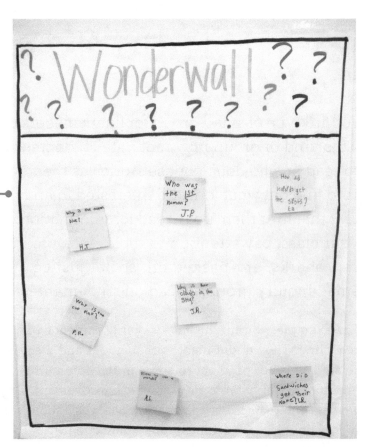

Wonder Wall where kids post their questions for inquiry.

- Here are some tried-and-true ways to tap into kids' curiosity. Follow a webcam. Children will love observing eagles, pandas, gorillas, and other animals in zoos and in the wild, for example. As you watch together for three to five minutes, have kids jot down observations and questions they have and then share these in small groups. For a list of twenty-five kid-friendly webcam sites, check out https://www.weareteachers.com/best-nature-webcams.

- Take students on brief virtual field trips to places they are interested in, such as the White House, the Grand Canyon, or Disneyland. Use Google Earth to see what these locations look like and remind students to jot questions as they arise.

- Introduce inquiry with a Genius Hour. This movement was inspired by businesses like Google that give employees an hour each week to follow their passions to explore novel ideas or work on new skills of their choice. Start small and establish a strong structure to help kids be successful. Check out these ten questions answered about Genius Hour: https://www.cultofpedagogy.com/genius-hour-questions.

Asking Questions

After students ask questions while watching a webcam or going on a virtual field trip, have them work in small groups to decide if a question is open-ended or close-ended. This will help them learn to ask deeper questions for inquiry. They might write C or O in front of each question they asked. Teach them the difference between these kinds of questions:

CLOSE-ENDED QUESTIONS	OPEN-ENDED QUESTIONS
Can be answered with one word or phrase	Can be answered in your own words with your own thinking
Can often be answered with *yes* or *no*	Have lots of different answers
Often begin with *did* or *will*	Often begin with *why, how,* or *what*
	Are good for deeper inquiry

Model how to ask questions as you contribute to a Wonder Wall. A website like Wonderopolis (https://wonderopolis.org) can serve as a model with its daily questions and related articles. Designate time—like Wonderopolis Wednesdays—devoted to exploring the question of the day and showing students how to dig deeper. This may give kids ideas of topics they want to explore. It's an opportunity to do shared reading with informational text, too.

The Frayer model often used in word study can be a great tool for inquiry. For example, early in the year (or anytime you decide to start inquiry groups) you might have kids do Frayer-a-Friend using a template adapted from https://www.eduprotocols.com. Pair students and have them interview each other by asking questions such as *What are four things you like? What are four things you don't like?* They can also draw or take photos to share information. This mini-inquiry gives kids opportunities to ask questions, get to know each other, and review how to use tech tools. It can also provide a starting point to learn about your students' interests. A printable can be found in the online companion, **resources.corwin.com/simplysmallgroups**.

When students are beginning any other inquiry, they can use the Frayer to record their questions and any information they find related to their topic. A printable Frayer-a-Topic template is available in the online companion at **resources.corwin.com/simplysmallgroups**, and an example follows.

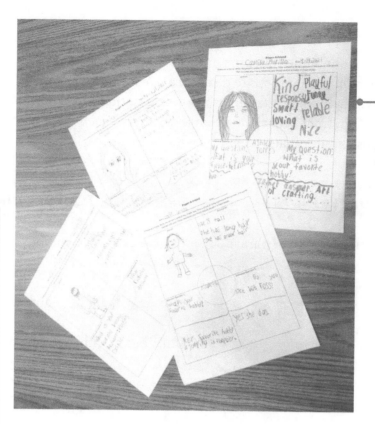

Frayer-a-Friend is used to help kids ask questions and get to know each other and their interests.

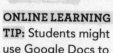

ONLINE LEARNING TIP: Students might use Google Docs to work together to create their Frayer-a-Friend. Use Padlet or Google Classroom to share their work with the class and build community. Keep it simple!

Frayer-a-Topic helps students organize their thinking around a new topic they'd like to explore.

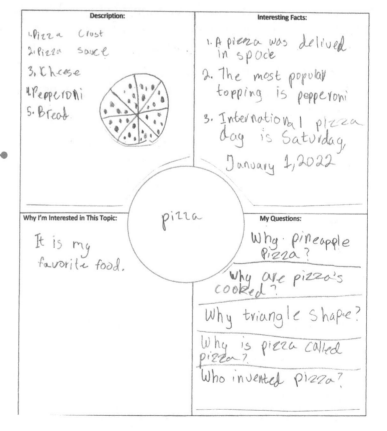

Organizing for Inquiry

Students will need a folder or notebook for storing materials used during inquiry. A pocket folder with brads can help them organize their notes. Or they might glue recording sheets and use sticky notes in a notebook. Let them decorate their folder or notebook with images related to their topic to increase interest and engagement. Students could also create a Google folder online.

Fluent readers take notes about glaciers using a Chromebook and a tree map as part of an inquiry group.

As students engage in their inquiry, they will need to take notes. An Inquiry Chart can be a helpful support; a printable is provided in the online companion. Model how to take simple notes through words or sketches and record the source as kids read related texts, view videos, or interview experts.

Images may be used in the final stage of their inquiry as students share what they learned with others. Discuss copyright and fair use, too, so children understand the rules and ethics about using images. For instance, they might use stock photos or clipart. But if they use Google Images, show them how to click on Tools and select Creative Commons Licenses to ensure the photos they use are within the boundaries of copyright law. Students may also take their own photos.

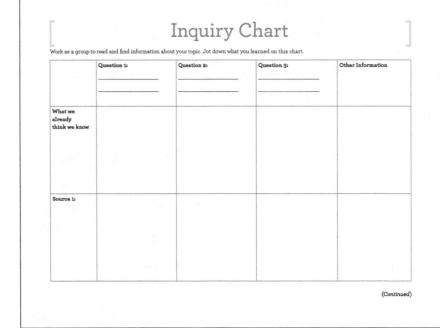

Inquiry Chart

Work as a group to read and find information about your topic. Jot down what you learned on this chart.

	Question 1: _____ _____	Question 2: _____ _____	Question 3: _____ _____	Other Information
What we already think we know				
Source 1:				

(Continued)

ONLINE LEARNING TIP: Teach students how to create an electronic file of images they might use as they share what they learned in their inquiry group.

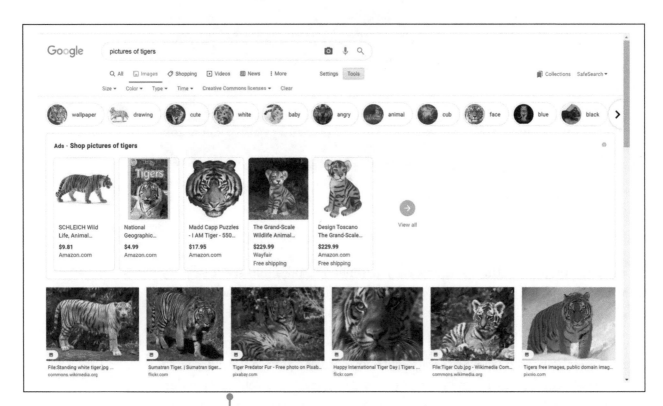

Screenshot of Google Images and Creative Commons Licenses tab of pictures of tigers kids might use when reporting what they learned.

Meeting in Inquiry Groups

As inquiry begins, be sure to build on what students already know about a topic. This will develop deeper understanding as you build from known to new information. Sometimes kids think they know something, yet their facts are not actually true. As children share what they know, help them be flexible by stating this is what we *think* we know now. Gently help them undo confusions that may arise. You might use the Truth or Lie series of informational books for kids to learn to evaluate information carefully. This series from Step Into Reading has books on sharks, dinosaurs, inventors, and presidents.

After students have researched a topic, help them plan a project or action to share or apply what they learned.

A graphic organizer, such as the KWL (Know-Wonder-Learn) or a variation, can aid students in their inquiry. These organizers help students build on background knowledge and organize new knowledge as its acquired.

Students use technology and sticky notes on a KWL chart to investigate a topic of interest.

ONLINE LEARNING TIP: Use Kahoot to play Two Truths and a Lie. A group of students could even create their own using information from an inquiry they did.

The chart below details how an inquiry group for fluent readers might operate with accompanying teacher roles.

	HOW AN INQUIRY GROUP WORKS	TEACHER ROLE
GETTING STARTED	1. Form a group based on student interest. Set up an inquiry folder or notebook.	Use observation and Frayer-a-Friend to form groups. You might start with pairs and later build to groups of three to five students. Give each student an inquiry folder or notebook to store their materials.
	2. Meet as a group to discuss what you know about the topic. Always bring your folder or notebook to meetings.	Be a member of the group to start. Introduce Frayer-a-Topic. Kids in the group should work with the same topic (e.g., planes, football, recycling). Have them fill in the topic, description, four interesting facts, and why I'm interested in this topic. Have them jot down questions they have, too.
	3. Read or view information related to the topic. Jot down questions to prepare for the next meeting.	Provide an article to read or a video for students to watch related to their topic. Model how to write an open-ended question in response to what they read or watched. Then have kids read/view and write questions independently.
	4. Meet to discuss what you read and share questions about the topic. Set up an Inquiry Chart for taking notes.	Lead a discussion and have each kid share questions they generated. Help them evaluate which are open- or close-ended. Then have them work together to choose their top four questions as a group. Model how to set up an Inquiry Chart and take notes.

Simply Small Groups

	HOW AN INQUIRY GROUP WORKS	TEACHER ROLE
READ AND COLLECT INFORMATION	5. Read on your own or with a partner and collect information.	Provide texts (print and online) related to the topic that might help answer students' questions.
	6. Meet to discuss what you read. Compare ideas. Refine questions, as needed.	Guide the group in the beginning. Students might meet once or twice a week.
	7. Repeat steps 5 and 6.	Be part of the group as long as needed. Then just drop in to visit and listen to students' discussion.
SHARE WHAT YOU LEARNED: PROJECT OR ACTION	8. Design an action or project related to your inquiry.	Help students think about how they might share what they learned through a project or action.
	9. Continue meeting to work on the project or action.	Provide support as needed. Help kids gather or organize resources. Put them in touch with experts.
	10. Share the final results. Reflect on your inquiry.	Help kids publish what they learned and share it with others at school, home, and in the community. Guide their reflection.

Reading and Taking Notes

Students need models of how to take notes before we can expect them to do this on their own. No wonder kids often just want to copy the exact words from a text! (Teach them that this is called plagiarism and is unethical and a violation of copyright law. Learning means synthesizing information and putting it into your own words.)

Start by having kids view a video or listen to a recording to take notes as part of your inquiry group. Make an anchor chart to help kids remember how to take notes. Pictured on the next page are a few charts from my book *Simply Stations: Listening and Speaking*. (See pages 116–133 of that book for lessons and ideas on how to teach kids to take notes.)

Take NOTES

- 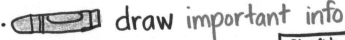 for repeated words (starfish, starfish, starfish)

- for pictures

- draw important info

- add labels

Sample anchor chart on how to take notes in primary grades.

Another anchor chart on how to take notes in intermediate grades.

How to Take NOTES

1. Use the **title** & **headings** for **BIG IDEAS**.

2. Listen/look for repeated words & ideas.   *don't plagiarize/copy*

3. Jot down a few words.

4. Make lists with titles

Hailey Richman
- 9 years old
- grandma is ill
- helps in nursing home

to help you remember important information.

5. Or use maps.

ill grand... / Hailey Richman / 9 yr. old / helps in nursing home
web

Hailey Richman		
9 yr. old NYC	grandma is ill	helps in homes

tree map

Other ideas to scaffold students' understanding of notetaking include the following:

- Take notes together and compare what everyone in the group thinks is important. Help students listen for repeated words and ideas and specific answers to their questions. Have them pay attention to the visuals, too, including photos, illustrations, diagrams, and other text features like bold words and headings.

- Model how to read a section, stop and jot, and then move to another section. When searching for answers to inquiry questions, show how to use the table of contents and index to locate information. Emphasize just jotting down bits of information to capture an idea or key point, not whole sentences.

- Teach children how to do sketch notes. This technique, created by Mike Rohde, frees up the reader (or listener) to take notes using just a few words and quick sketches. Check out this short video from Rohde covering the basics and the rationale behind visual notetaking, and consider showing kids a segment (from timecode 9:51 to 14:00) for a simple demonstration of how to sketch with just five shapes: https://bit.ly/2OEnfCL.

EL TIP: Multilingual learners might start by brainstorming words around the topic to develop vocabulary. Have them use one color for English and another color for their home language. Then look for patterns.

Reflection to Wrap Up Inquiry

Including reflection as part of small group can help learning stick. Have a final meeting with your inquiry group and help students think about the process they engaged in, what they learned, and what they might do differently for the next inquiry. You don't have to grade the work that students did! Instead, invite students to self-evaluate. You'll find a sample reflection sheet in the online companion at **resources.corwin.com/simplysmallgroups**.

More Inquiry Group Ideas

- Use what your class is studying in social studies or science to build curiosity and develop inquiry questions. This helps kids develop background knowledge that is needed for inquiry. Post questions kids come up with on your Wonder Wall.

- Place text sets (books about the same topic) in your classroom library with labels created by students. Ask kids to add to these to develop ownership. For example, you might have a basket of books about hurricanes, especially during hurricane season. Or you might put together a collection of books about football in the weeks leading up to the Super Bowl. If you notice that students have been talking about an event in the news, find articles and books about that topic for them to explore further.

- Many students are interested in video games. Instead of dismissing this as nonacademic, help kids explore this topic and hone their research skills. For example, help students discover the story within a video game. Their questions might be "What is the story in this video game? What are the characters' strengths and weaknesses? What is the setting? How is the plot developed?" Or have students explore the origin of a video game with questions such as "Who created this video game? What skills did this person need? How do you code? How did the game maker learn to do this?" They could interview video game creators. As a project to share what they learned, students might create their own world and a challenge as the seeds of their own video game. What students are learning could be content for their YouTube channel someday!

- Activist work is another avenue to pursue related to inquiry. Students might use a current event or crisis to formulate questions and respond in ways that change behavior. For example, an inquiry on "How can we stay safe at school?" might lead to kids making signs and writing letters to administrators or government officials. The question "What foods are the healthiest for kids?" might lead to a campaign for locally grown plants to be used in school lunches and snacks. To get kids interested, you might show students short video clips on kids who are activists. Have your students listen for what this person was passionate about. What problem did they identify? How did they bring about change? Search for pieces with the child activist talking at the ages listed below. Here are a few suggestions:

  - **Marley Dias**: A young Black girl who began a social media campaign for #1000BlackGirlBooks at age ten and wrote a book at age twelve, *Marley Dias Gets It Done—And So Can You*

  - **Mari Copeny** (a.k.a. Little Miss Flint): An eight-year-old Black girl who wrote a letter to President Barack Obama about the water crisis in her city of Flint, Michigan, and began a bottled water campaign to distribute over a million bottles of water to her community

  - **Xiuhtezcati Martinez**: A Native American male who spoke publicly at age six about saving our earth and today is a hip-hop artist and youth director of Earth Guardians, a worldwide conservation organization

  - **Sophie Cruz**: A five-year-old who ran past a barricade in Washington, D.C., and shared a message with Pope Francis about her undocumented immigrant family from Oaxaca, Mexico, and continues to fight for immigrant rights today

  - **Bana al-Abed**: A seven-year-old Syrian girl who sent Twitter messages (with help from her English-speaking mom) documenting the war in her city of Aleppo and calling for peace; she later published a memoir, *Dear World*

EL TIP: Creating a brochure using digital tools, images, and short bits of text is a fun way for multilingual learners to communicate what they learned about a topic.

- Invite students to share what they learned in creative ways to culminate their inquiry. Show kids ideas and invite them to create their own. Here are a few to get you started:

  ○ Make a mind map. Use words and images to show what you learned. Write your question in a circle in the middle and draw spokes coming from the circle. On each line, write something you learned and add a drawing. You might use different colors to show related ideas.

  ○ Create a video showcasing what you learned. Model how to make a plan first! Some students might enjoy watching the information put together by three young girls on how to make a video: https://bit.ly/3cojiKy.

  ○ Publish a short informational text about your findings. Incorporate text features and text structures.

  ○ Record an interview with your group telling what you learned.

  ○ Compose a poem or song that gives answers to your questions.

  ○ Make a poster or model illustrating what you learned.

  ○ Design a museum exhibit showcasing your findings.

  ○ Develop three truths and a lie pages around your topic. Use related books from the Steps to Reading series as a model.

Writing Groups

One more small group option for fluent readers is a writing group. Writing is typically a solitary act and can feel lonely and even overwhelming at times. Being a member of a writing group can motivate you to become a better writer, inspire you with new ideas for writing, and help you improve your craft.

Keep the writing group fun, so kids will want to be a part of it. Write alongside your students and provide a model for being a writer. Share your writing life with your children! Show them your notebooks, the kind of pen or pencil you like to write with, or the digital device you use as a writer.

You might use the name "writing clubs" instead of "writing groups" and run them in a similar fashion as the twenty-minute book clubs described on pages 215–218. Start with an invitation to the class to join a writing group and let students choose to participate. This will give you a chance to try this type of group with willing members. Their enthusiasm will be contagious and may get more reluctant writers to sign up eventually. Make your writing groups feel more like a VIP club, and kids will be begging to join you!

Establish a Safe, Supportive Environment for Writers

Writing is hard work. It involves risk-taking as you put your thoughts and ideas on paper and then speak your words into existence by sharing them with others. It's important to create an environment where kids feel safe to express themselves both verbally and in writing. Be a model by writing alongside your kids and experiencing the same things they are trying. Create a sense of trust and belonging. Listen to your students and get to know them. Find out their strengths and build on their interests. Share and show empathy. Tune into what's hard for them, too, and lend support.

Acknowledge the work kids are doing as writers. Thank them for trying new things and doing their best. Something as simple as, "Thanks for leaving spaces between your words. It made it really easy for me to read your writing and understand your message." Or "You worked hard to add details. They really help us picture what you were going through."

Share stories about characters that take risks to build that trait in your students. You might read aloud short picture books, such as *Courage* by Bernard Waber or *Raccoon on His Own* by Jim Arnosky. Acknowledge when kids take risks as writers. Instead of saying "I like the way . . ." say "You took a risk as a writer by . . . How did that feel?"

Types of Writing Groups

There are a variety of ways to form groups for writing. Some might meet for several weeks; others might only meet a time or two. Here are several types of writing groups you might try:

- **Genre group.** Students work to write and improve pieces within one genre. This can be a great way to examine the characteristics of genre. You might have a Poetry Writing Group or a Group That Writes Graphic Novels. Lead a discussion about genre characteristics and then have kids listen for those in each other's pieces as they share.

- **Idea-generating group.** These kids come together to brainstorm ideas of what they might write about. They may make lists or heart maps and share these with each other. Or they may take turns telling stories to help them come up with ideas of what they can write about.

- **Feedback group.** Kids who are writing and want feedback come to this kind of writing group. They take turns sharing what they are writing and have peers listen, question, and comment. Then writers revise based on that feedback and share again. Keep the group small so everyone can share.

- **Word-lover group.** Invite students who want to improve their word choice to this kind of group. Examine well-written pieces of text from favorite authors. You might take just one page and have kids discuss the author's word choice and what they learn from this. Then have kids help each other look at a piece of their writing and work together to revise using more descriptive language. Provide reference tools like thesauruses and dictionaries for kids to use.

- **Mechanics group.** There may be some kids who want help with spelling or using punctuation. You can have a group that focuses on improving mechanics to make it easier for others to read their writing. Be sure to celebrate their message or content before delving into spelling, grammar, or using periods.

- **Favorite author group.** Invite kids who like a particular author to meet and study that person as a writer. Visit some of the author's books and discuss what makes the writing work. View or read author interviews. What resonates with your students? Why do they like this author? What can they try in their own writing? Students might even work together to write a letter or email to this author telling what they like or asking questions. Address the correspondence to the author via the publisher and eagerly expect a response.

Choosing What to Focus On

It will be helpful to have a focus for your writing group. As described in the previous examples, you might form a group based on a need. Or you may choose a focus based on what you notice about kids' writing in the group from the last time they met. Pick just one or two things for students to work on or listen for in a small group writing session. Post the focus on a dry erase board to help students pay attention and improve one aspect of their writing at a time.

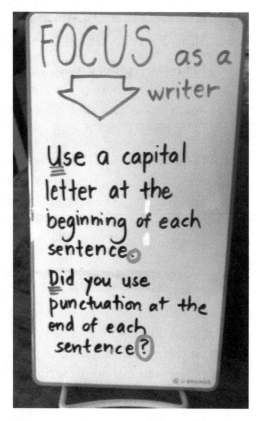

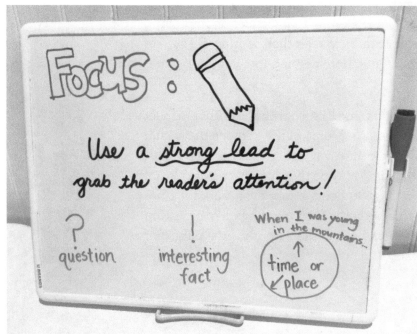

ONLINE LEARNING TIP: Ahead of time send kids information on what they need for upcoming small group meetings. Include the lesson focus along with a link to what they'll read. If you have a dry erase board behind you when on camera, post your focus there, too, for students to see.

Meeting in Writing Groups

This is how a writing group for fluent readers might operate with accompanying teacher roles.

HOW WRITING GROUPS WORK	TEACHER ROLE
1. Form a group.	Use a sign-up sheet with limited numbers of spaces for a particular type of group. Start with the type of group you feel will appeal the most to your students and will benefit them.
2. Do a fun warm-up related to writing or word play.	Be the timekeeper (or have a student do this) so the game doesn't take up the entire small group time.
3. Establish ground rules for the group. Decide when to meet and how often you will meet.	Create a list of expectations with kids in the group. Focus on privacy, trying new things, giving feedback, and sharing. See the sample that follows. Display a class calendar to show when groups meet.
4. Choose a focus for the group.	Post the focus on a dry erase board and have kids find examples of this in their writing (or in model texts).
5. Share your writing. Look for examples related to the focus.	Lead the group and be sure everyone who wants to share has an opportunity. Help kids stick to the ground rules as they listen and give feedback.
6. Return to today's focus and summarize what you did.	Keep kids on track by returning to the focus and having students tell what they will try because of meeting in the writing group today.
7. Decide when to meet again and continue to write. Plan to bring new writing to the next meeting.	Help students make plans and get dates on the calendar. Note the group's goal here, too.
8. Meet again as a writing group and repeat steps 4–7.	Be an active part of this group, but let kids lead as much as possible. Support students as writers.

Writing Group Agreements

- Write before we meet.
- Be respectful. Be kind.
- Take risks. Try new things as writers.
- Ask for feedback.
- Help each other.
- HAVE FUN!

Sample of ground rules created by a writing group.

ONLINE LEARNING TIP: Play Bananagrams online at https://www.playbananagrams.com. Or, play old-school Boggle remotely by using a document camera to project the tray with letter cubes for online players to see. Have them use a pencil and paper to write down all the words they find in the allotted time.

Fun Things for Kids to Do in Writing Groups

You might start your writing group with a fun warm-up. Invite kids to create their own unique ways to start the group, too. Join in with them! Here are few ideas to try:

- To get kids thinking about words, you might play a quick round of a word-related board game, such as the following:

  - Bananagrams

  - Boggle

  - Apples to Apples

  - Taboo, Jr.

- Start with a joke. Knock-knock jokes are often favorites! Or read a pun or riddle. Invite kids to bring their own to the next meeting.

- To get the creative juices going, make up a group story. The first person starts the story with something like, "One day a black cat ran across the playground." The next child adds another sentence. The student beside that student adds another sentence until everyone has had a chance to participate. The whole exercise is oral. Telling a story can help with writing a story! Set a timer for three minutes. When it rings, that person ends the story.

- Have everyone tell a sentence related to an emotion. Pick one at a time, such as *happiness*, *fear*, *surprise*, or *embarrassment*. It can be as simple as, "I was so happy the day my braces came off. The first thing I did was bite into an apple," or "My face broke into a huge smile when my dad walked into the house with baby rabbits!" Go around the circle inviting each child to say a sentence or two.

- Write Three-Minute Three-Word Poems to play with language. Choose three words and write them on a dry erase board. Each group member has three minutes to write a poem using all three words. Just have fun with it! It can be silly or serious. Invite students to share their poems.

- Play Pass the List. Each student in the group gets a long, skinny piece of list paper. Have kids label their paper with any title they choose and list one item that matches. For example, the title might be *Farm Animals* and they list *cow*. Then have them fold over the paper to hide the title and just show the first item on the list. Everyone passes their paper to the person on their left and adds one item to the list, trying to guess what the list is about. Continue until everyone has written on each list. Then have the group guess what the title of each list is and show the titles.

ONLINE LEARNING TIP: Adapt Pass the List for online play. Here's how:

1. Give each student in the small group a number (from 1 to 5 if you have five students). Each student types their number at the top of their own Google Doc and thinks of a topic. Then they type an item that matches that topic under their number.

2. Next, students share their documents with each other. Everyone takes turns adding another word to each list, trying to guess what the topic is by writing other things that match. For example, a student might add drum or trumpet to a list that starts with guitar.

3. When everyone has had a chance to add a word to every list, the group guesses the title of each list. In the example above, it might be Instruments. The originator of each list tells if the others guessed their topic correctly.

EL TIP: Playing word games and making up oral stories with multilingual students can be fun and creates a positive atmosphere. Laughing and learning together can help kids feel more comfortable when acquiring a new language.

Providing Feedback to Others as Writers

It's important to teach kids how to give feedback to other writers. Begin by having one-on-one conferences with students during writing workshop. The more comfortable you are with giving feedback to writers, the better you will be able to model this invaluable skill.

Meet with your writing group and make a chart of writing goals students are working on. (See the example on the facing page.) Have kids use this list to give specific feedback to each other. Then model how to give and receive feedback. Have one student be the author and the other the editor. (Printables of Author and Editor signs are available online at **resources.corwin.com/ simplysmallgroups** for kids to use.) The author reads a piece of writing to the editor. The editor listens and then gives feedback. The author then makes changes to the writing with help from the editor if requested. Then students switch roles.

Here is a sample exchange from a small group working on adding details to help the reader visualize:

Author: (reads piece)

Editor: (tells something positive and specific to the group's target goals) *I could really picture the setting of your story. The details about the weather outside made me feel like I was there.*

Author: *Thank you.* (names what they did) *I tried using adjectives that described how cold it was outside that day.*

Editor: (asks a question) *Who else was there with you? I was trying to figure that part out. Maybe some more details would help.*

Author: *My mom was along. I will add some more about her and the part she played in my story.*

Editor: *Would you like to add that now? I'd love to listen to your story again after you're done with that part.*

Author: *Ok. Thanks for your feedback.*

Chart of small group writing goals.

You might also help your group make a list of expectations for giving writing feedback. See the example in the photo.

Tips for Giving Writing Feedback chart.

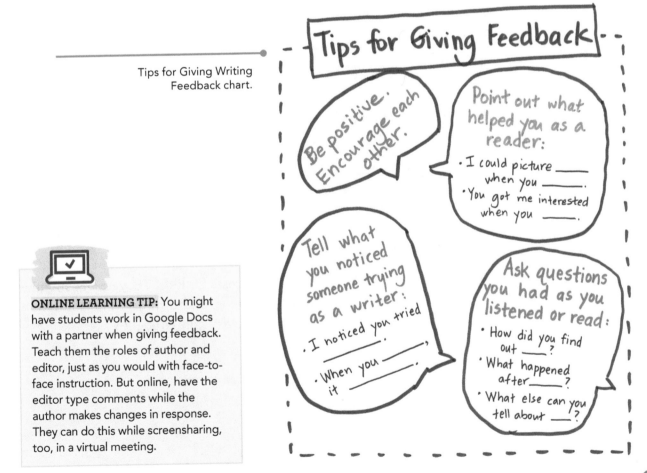

ONLINE LEARNING TIP: You might have students work in Google Docs with a partner when giving feedback. Teach them the roles of author and editor, just as you would with face-to-face instruction. But online, have the editor type comments while the author makes changes in response. They can do this while screensharing, too, in a virtual meeting.

Publishing Students' Writing

While working in small groups, keep publication in mind. It's fun for students to have their small group members as an audience. But offer the option to expand their audience to an even larger one. Some students may want to work toward publication of a piece in an online or print journal. Here are a few sites that publish work by elementary children:

- *New Moon Girls* is a monthly magazine for girls by girls, ages eight to fourteen. https://newmoongirls.com/girls-get-published

- *Magic Dragon* is a beautiful magazine with writing and art by children ages twelve and under. It is published quarterly. You can view submission guidelines here: http://www.magicdragonmagazine.com/?page_id=1109

- *Skipping Stones* is an online magazine that publishes writing by children ages seven to eighteen. Kids can submit poems, stories, artwork, essays, and photo essays. Click here for information on youth submissions: http://www.skippingstones.org/wp/youth

- Stone Soup originated in 1973 and is written by kids for kids ages thirteen and under. To submit work, go to https://stonesoup.com/how-to-submit-writing-and-art-to-stone-soup

You might also keep an eye open for writing contests for kids. Here are a few to get you started:

- *Cricket Magazine* poetry contest: http://www.cricketmagkids.com/contests#show

- Some PBS stations have writing contests for students in Grades K–5. Here's one: https://www.wqed.org/education/writers-contest

- The Geek Partnership Experience is a nonprofit group that runs writing contests for people of all ages. Students can submit science fiction, fantasy, horror, supernatural, and alternate history pieces in the form of short fiction, poetry, or comics. For more information, visit https://geekpartnership.org/programs/writing-contest

- Story Monsters Ink has writing contests for kids. They accept submissions, including articles, essays, poems, or drawings, from children in Grades K–12: https://www.storymonsters.com/student-writer

[If You See This, Try This ...]

Regardless of the kind of small groups you use with fluent readers, it's important to look at what students *can* do. Although students at this level are fluent, sometimes they may get stuck along the developmental continuum. Here are some specific solutions to common sticking points for fluent readers.

IF YOU SEE THIS ...	TRY THIS:
Can read but chooses not to	• Focus on reading motivation. • Use book clubs and opportunities to talk with others about books read.
Frequently abandons books	• Find out *why* they didn't finish those books. Have kids keep a list of abandoned books and jot down what kept them from reading the whole book. Then help students look for patterns and find books that better meet their needs.
Gets frustrated when encountering long words and just makes stuff up	• Say, "You're using some of the sounds and making up a word. Stop doing that. Look at the word. Read the sounds (or parts) in order. Be sure the word makes sense."

(Continued)

(*Continued*)

IF YOU SEE THIS . . .	TRY THIS:
Always reads the same genre or rereads the same books over and over	<ul><li>You might use book clubs with new genres and invite kids to join. Do a convincing preview of a book in the new genre to get students interested.</li><li>Introduce a new genre in guided reading to get kids trying something new.</li><li>Have students do book previews to entice others to read new things.</li><li>Help kids set the goal, "Read a new genre." Perhaps make November or March "Read a New Genre Month."</li></ul>
Chooses books that are too easy	<ul><li>Try to find out why. Then help them find texts that interest them and are at a slightly higher reading level.</li><li>Share your reading life with them. Model how you read some easier *and* some more challenging things.</li><li>Have students make recordings of these books for students in lower grades to use. This will help them focus on reading with expression and may encourage rereading for new purposes.</li></ul>
Oral reading lacks expression or fluency	<ul><li>Model how to read a line or two with expression. Then have kids echo read to sound like you. You might teach them how to record their reading of a page so they can listen and hear their expression.</li><li>They might make recordings for students in lower grades to use.</li></ul>

IF YOU SEE THIS . . .	TRY THIS:
Speed reads without deep comprehension (to be the first to finish)	• If meeting in guided reading, have students read just a bit and take notes (to slow down their reading and increase comprehension). • Meeting in book clubs can help students focus more on comprehension. It doesn't matter if they finish first; they have to understand what they read to fully participate in a book club.
Reads much better than they write	• Build on students' reading strengths as they learn to grow their writing. Help kids study favorite authors in a writing group and try what they're learning in their own writing.
Can write but chooses not to	• Joining a writing group might help. Writing with others can be motivating as kids share with peers. Working toward publication or for a specific purpose may motivate some. • Help students with the mechanics of writing, as needed. Some may need a pencil grip to hold a pencil comfortably; others may need keyboarding practice. • Offer different tools for writing, such as gel pens or skinny markers. • Provide a variety of paper options. Graph paper may help some children with spacing.

Reflection and Printable Tools

This section is designed to provide a visual index of everything you need to work successfully in small groups throughout the school year. All the printable materials can be downloaded from the online companion, located at **resources .corwin.com/simplysmallgroups**.

resources.corwin.com/
simplysmallgroups

We start with questions to use for personal **reflection**, things to discuss in Professional Learning Community (PLC) or data team meetings with your grade level, and questions for students to use when thinking about their work in small groups.

Next, you'll find **printable planning tools** for small groups: weekly scheduling charts and simple lesson templates. There are charts to help you think about reading levels and what to focus on at different reading stages, as well as who will be in those groups.

Finally, there are thumbnails of **printable teaching tools**. These are organized by reading stages to make it easy to locate what you need to teach in small groups—from high-frequency word lists for emergent readers to questions for book clubs and inquiry groups for fluent readers.

I'd love to hear from you about the tools you use for small group literacy instruction, too. Please use the hashtag #simplysmallgroups on social media. You can find me online at the following:

@debbiediller (Twitter)

debbie.diller (Instagram)

dillerdebbie (Facebook)

www.debbiediller.com (website)

Reflection Tools

Here are some questions to reflect on across the school year, after you've been working with your students in small group for a while. The online companion website, **resources.corwin.com/ simplysmallgroups**, contains printables of reflection tools for teacher use, PLC use, and student use following small group time. Use these pages to record what you've tried, what's worked, and what you might change in the future. I recommend making three copies of this reflection sheet and filling it in at the beginning, middle, and end of the school year, or at the end of each term.

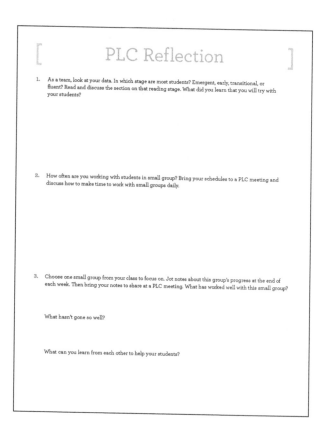

Student Reflection Cards

I recommend that you save about five to ten minutes each day for a whole class Reflection Time after small group. Have your students meet in the whole group meeting area and talk with them about what they learned during small group or at a few stations they worked at that day. This will provide paperless accountability and lets children know you care about what they practiced and learned today. It also will help you troubleshoot and provide ongoing positive reminders about what to do at stations to prevent interruptions at the small group table.

You won't have time to ask every student to share every day. So, choose a few kids to reflect each day. I recommend starting with children who need a celebration or those who tried something that will benefit others in the classroom. Try to include all students within a two-week period.

If you choose not to have whole group Reflection Time, you can use a reflection card at the end of a small group lesson before students leave the table. Give them a minute to talk about what they learned and how they will apply this as readers or writers.

What follows is a thumbnail of a printable reflection card to use *after* small group time. There is one card for each developmental reading stage. My Simply Stations books each contain printable reflection cards to use after stations time. Feel free to use those cards for student Reflection Time, too.

HOW to USE REFLECTION CARDS

1. Gather your class to the carpet following small group time and stations for Reflection Time.

2. Choose a few students to share something they learned in small group today (or at stations).

3. Use a reflection card to guide the discussion.

4. Ask one or two questions from the card.

5. Repeat the following day with different students sharing.

Emergent Readers
1. Show a new word you learned to read or write in small group today.
2. Tell about a book you read or talked about in small group today.
3. Tell something you learned in small group today.

Printable Planning Tools

As noted in Section 1, it's important to determine and understand each student's stage of reading and language development when planning for small group instruction. You probably have children reading at a variety of levels, and those levels will change throughout the school year. Be ready to adjust instruction in small groups based on what you know about your kids and their stages of development.

The companion website, **resources.corwin.com/simplysmallgroups**, contains printable tools to help you while planning for differentiated instruction all year long. You may want to print and keep them at the front of your small group teaching binder for quick reference. Here's what you'll find online and how you might use these tools:

1. Determine each student's reading stage.

Use the **How to Determine the Child's Developmental Reading Stage** chart as you begin thinking about small group instruction. Listen to each child read and have a brief discussion. Read through the hallmarks of each stage to decide which phase best matches each student. Then form small groups accordingly. Matching reading levels can be found at the bottom of this chart.

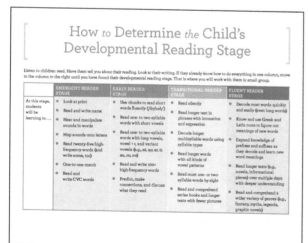

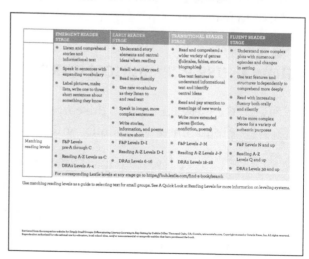

Simply Small Groups

A Quick Look at Reading Levels is a double-page synopsis of several popular reading level systems. This chart will help you understand why there's not a simple correlation between all of these. You might read about the leveling system your school uses and compare it to others you've heard about. There are links from each publisher to research more about each system.

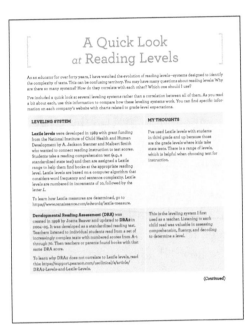

A Simple Look at Language Acquisition is a chart designed to help you think about children's language levels if you have students learning English as a new language. There are simple suggestions for supporting language development when planning and teaching in small groups. Use this chart along with EL tips found throughout this book.

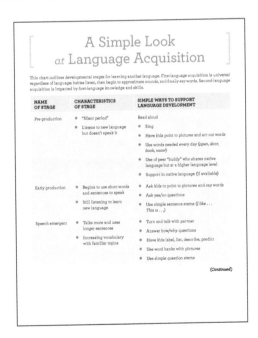

2. Form groups and learn about key reading behaviors for each stage.

Keep the **Key Reading Behaviors** charts, one for each reading stage from emergent to fluent, at your fingertips when planning. Use these charts to help you choose a focus for each small group.

Each chart lists the most important reading behaviors within a stage as children progress from one level to the next. Find and print the chart that matches the developmental stage of each of your groups. Then cut out the strip that matches each group's level. Attach it to your small group's folder with Velcro dots or paper clips as shown on page 21. Use the strips to determine what you will focus on in a small group lesson. See the corresponding developmental stage section in this book for teaching ideas.

You might make a second copy of a chart to use as a quick reference or overview. Place it at the front of your small group binder. Also share the chart in parent-teacher conferences to show family members what their child should work on and where they're headed next.

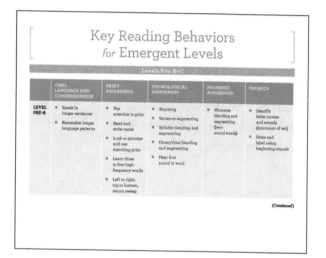

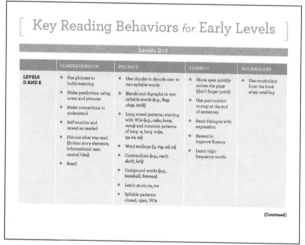

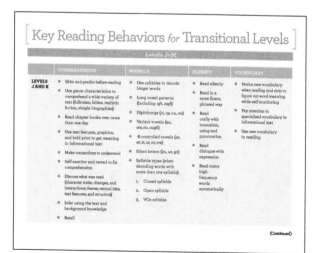

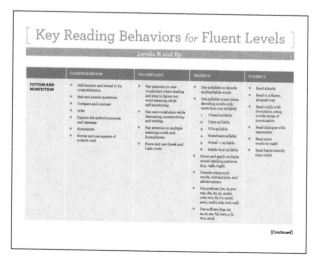

You may want to also print a copy of the **Teaching Tips** charts that match key reading behaviors for each stage as a quick reference to use while planning. These can be found online and are included in the text in Sections 2–5.

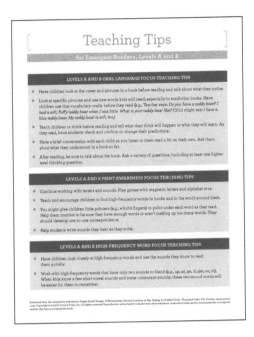

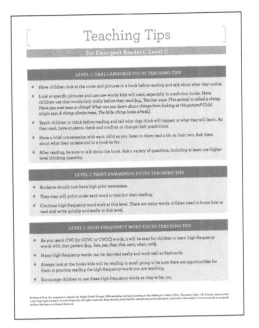

As you form groups, use the **Types of Small Groups and Who Will Be in Each** chart. Look at each option and decide who will best be served by this type of small group and why.

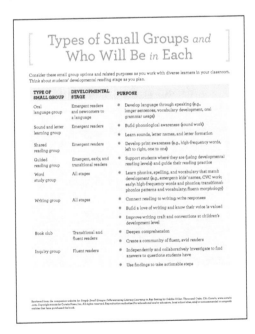

3. Make a small group schedule and teach expectations.

My Small Group Schedule for Two Weeks is a template to print and use to plan for each group across two weeks. You might use small sticky notes with a different color for each small group. Place sticky notes on the grid and move them around until you find a schedule that works. (If you are seeing two groups a day, you won't need the third row of the chart.)

There is also a **Checklist to Prevent Small Group Interruptions** with expectations to teach before teaching in small groups. Use this to keep track of modeling everything needed for kids to be successful while you are working with small groups.

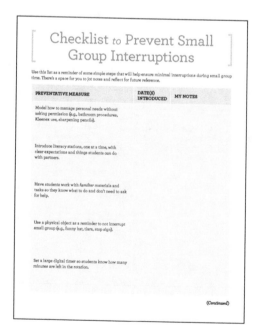

4. Begin planning small group lessons.

How to Plan a Small Group Lesson is a helpful tool to print and keep at the front of your small group binder. Use it as a reminder of steps to take when designing a lesson.

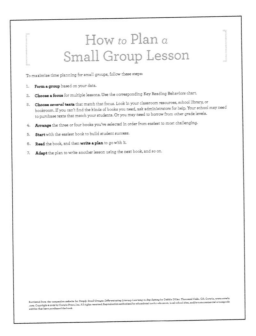

Diphthongs, variant vowels, vowel teams, syllable types? The printable reference, **Some Helpful Phonics Terms**, provides definitions to clarify phonics terms when planning for small groups. Print and keep this at the front of your small group binder, too.

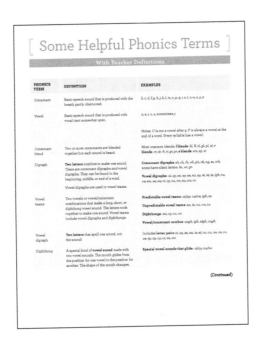

Use **Early Developmental Writing Stages** to help you design appropriate writing work when planning for small groups, especially at the emergent and early reading stages.

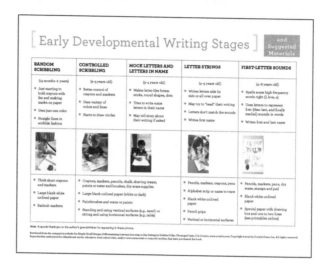

Print and fill out **Lesson Plan Templates** as you plan for each small group. You'll find a variety of reading and writing lesson plan templates for each stage of reading development, from emergent through fluent. Feel free to customize these to meet your needs.

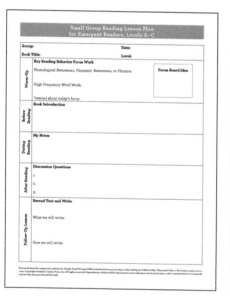
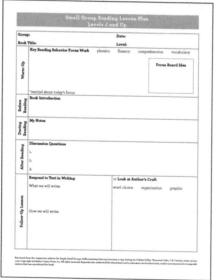

5. Use lesson ideas to focus your small group plans and accelerate students.

The last part of Section 6 includes **printable teaching tools** found in the online companion for each stage of reading development. These are from the **Focus Work** segments in Sections 2–5 and are provided to simplify your small group teaching.

Printable Teaching Tools

Emergent Readers (Section 2)

Focus Boards With Visuals for Emergent Readers will help kids know what you want them to take away from the small group lessons described in Section 2.

Print these and post the one that matches the day's lesson on your Focus Board. Or use these Focus Boards with visuals as a reference for your own designs. You will find one for each possible focus for small groups with emergent readers. They include images, since kids at this stage aren't reading much print. Stick with the same focus for multiple lessons.

I've curated a list of **Important High-Frequency Words for Emergent Readers** for you to use when selecting high-frequency words to teach emergent readers. I examined many books at each level and created lists of words used most often. Use this list as a starting point for choosing words for your Word Wall and related small group lessons. The online companion also includes **printable take-home lists for families** and a **Letter to the Family** with suggestions. Create your own lists based on the needs of your students, too.

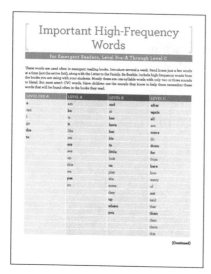

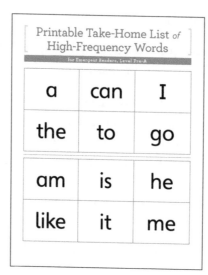

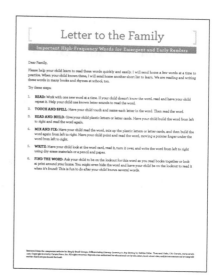

Guess the Word for Emergent Readers provides picture directions to help children practice reading and writing high-frequency words in a fun format. Use this printable to give clues to children as they work to develop sight vocabulary.

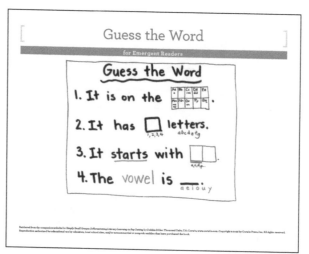

You'll find several printable **Nursery Rhymes** that contain high-frequency words highlighted in the list above. These large-print rhymes have high-frequency words in bold letters to provide a meaningful context for learning these words. Teach with these charts during whole and small group time and send them home for practice. Use them at a Nursery Rhyme or Poetry station, too.

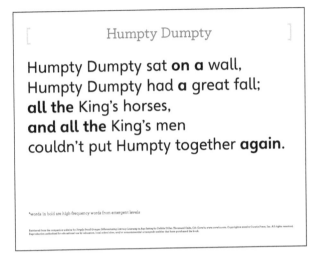

[Baa, Baa, Black Sheep]

Baa, baa, black sheep,
have you any wool?
Yes, sir, **yes**, sir.
Three bags full.
One **for my** master,
One **for my** dame,
And one **for the little** boy
who lives **down the** lane.

*words in bold are high-frequency words from emergent levels

Reprinted from the companion website for *Simply Small Groups: Differentiating Literacy Learning in Any Setting* by Debbie Diller. Thousand Oaks, CA: Corwin, www.corwin.com. Copyright 2022 by Corwin Press, Inc. All rights reserved. Reproduction authorized for educational use by educators, local school sites, and/or noncommercial or nonprofit entities that have purchased the book.

[Humpty Dumpty]

Humpty Dumpty sat **on a** wall,
Humpty Dumpty had **a** great fall;
all the King's horses,
and all the King's men
couldn't put Humpty together **again**.

*words in bold are high-frequency words from emergent levels

Reprinted from the companion website for *Simply Small Groups: Differentiating Literacy Learning in Any Setting* by Debbie Diller. Thousand Oaks, CA: Corwin, www.corwin.com. Copyright 2022 by Corwin Press, Inc. All rights reserved. Reproduction authorized for educational use by educators, local school sites, and/or noncommercial or nonprofit entities that have purchased the book.

Elkonin Box templates are useful for helping kids blend and segment sounds and matching letters. Use them with the accompanying phonological and CVC focus work in Section 2. These are excellent tools to share with families for at-home practice as well as at a Word Study station.

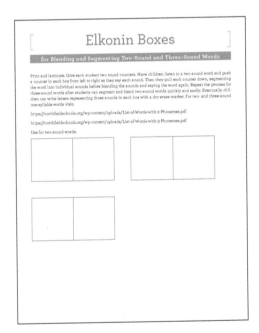

[Elkonin Boxes]

for Blending and Segmenting Two-Sound and Three-Sound Words

Print and laminate. Give each student two round counters. Have children listen to a two-sound word and push a counter in each box from left to right as they say each sound. Then they pull each counter down, segmenting the word into individual sounds before blending the sounds and saying the word again. Repeat the process for three-sound words after students can segment and blend two-sound words quickly and easily. Eventually children can write letters representing those sounds in each box with a dry erase marker. For two- and three-sound one-syllable words visit:

https://northfieldschools.org/wp-content/uploads/List-of-Words-with-2-Phonemes.pdf
https://northfieldschools.org/wp-content/uploads/List-of-Words-with-3-Phonemes.pdf

Use for two-sound words:

Sensory Talk Cards can be used to develop oral language with young children. Print them and use them with familiar objects and photos to help children use their senses to talk in longer and more developed sentences.

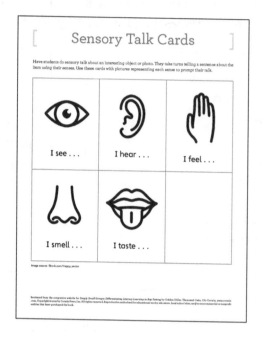

Early Readers (Section 3)

Many of the **Focus Boards With Visuals for Early Readers** relate to phonics focus work ideas from Section 3. Post one at a time on your Focus Board to help kids zero in on what you want them to try in today's lesson. Or use them as a springboard to create your own sketches and boards. Stick with a focus for multiple lessons until you see kids making progress.

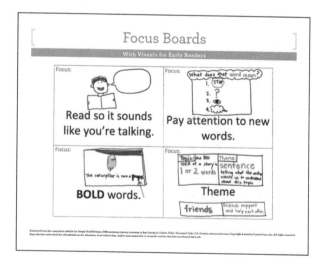

Several phonics tools are included. **Elkonin Box** templates are useful for helping students decode and write one-syllable words. Use them with the accompanying phonological and phonics focus work in Section 3. These are excellent tools to share with families for at-home practice as well as at a Word Study station. Sample **Blending Lines** are also included to help you plan phonics portions of small group lessons.

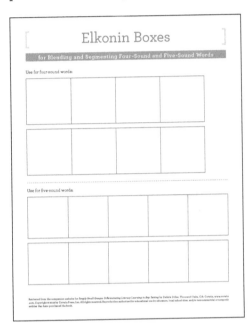

Elkonin Boxes

for Blending and Segmenting Four-Sound and Five-Sound Words

Use for four-sound words:

Use for five-sound words:

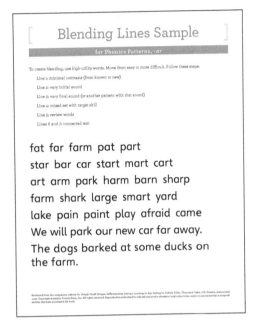

Blending Lines Sample

for Phonics Patterns, -ar

To create blending, use high-utility words. Move from easy to more difficult. Follow these steps:

Line 1: minimal contrasts (from known to new)

Line 2: vary initial sound

Line 3: vary final sound (or another pattern with that sound)

Line 4: mixed set with target skill

Line 5: review words

Lines 6 and 7: connected text

fat far farm pat part
star bar car start mart cart
art arm park harm barn sharp
farm shark large smart yard
lake pain paint play afraid came
We will park our new car far away.
The dogs barked at some ducks on
the farm.

Important High-Frequency Words for Early Readers is exactly that! There are many words for kids to learn at the early reader stage, so it's helpful to choose the ones that will be most needed at each reading level. As I read through many leveled books from a variety of publishers, I listed high-frequency words that appeared most often. This is not a definitive list, but you can use it as a starting point in choosing words for kids to practice until they know them by sight.

Important High-Frequency Words

for Early Readers, Levels D–I

Here is a list of words used often in books at the early reading stage. You might introduce three to five words a week, depending on your students' progress. I've included short printable lists to send home in the online companion, too. There is also a printable Letter to the Family. Work with words from the books your students are reading. Most of these are one- or two-syllable words. Help children use the sounds they know to help them remember these words that should match the books they are reading. I've typed the words in alphabetic order, but teach them in an order that matches your kids' needs. If these words aren't in the books you're using, adjust the list.

LEVELS D AND E	LEVELS F AND G	LEVELS H AND I
about	another	always
are	above	build
away	because	every
back	beside	everywhere
came	brother	found
could	busy	ground
day	carry	hungry
find	children	inside
give	each	laugh
help	eat	leave
house	happy	morning
how	father	once
into	friend	outside
make	full	people
more	good	together
new	know	upon
off	many	
over	mother	
put	never	

(Continued)

I've also included **printable take-home lists for families**. But feel free to create your own based on the needs of your students.

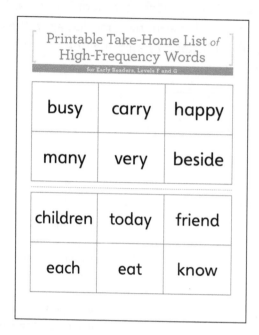

Guess the Word for Early Readers provides directions with visuals to help children practice reading and writing high-frequency words as they play a game. Print the directions and after students are familiar with the game, they may play it with a partner at a Word Study station using the Word Wall.

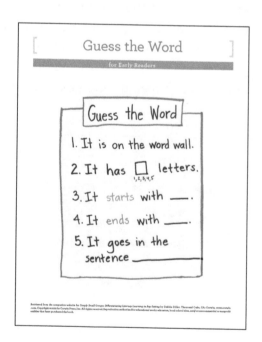

Printable **Nursery Rhymes** containing high-frequency words from the list on the facing page can be used for small group teaching. These rhymes have simple illustrations and high-frequency words in bold to anchor them. Kids can read nursery rhymes multiple times at school and home. You can create your own using this model, too. Don't forget to place these at your Poetry station for kids to practice!

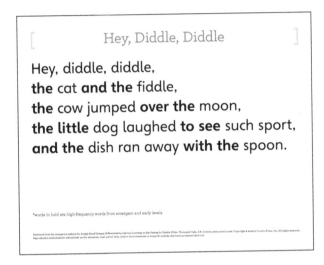

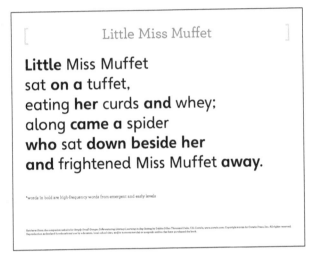

The **Retelling Fiction Strip** is an easy-to-use visual that will help early readers learn to retell. Print one for your small group to share. Provide students with this tool, too, as a take-home material. Have children point to each color and tell key details about what happened in the beginning, middle, and end of a story in small group. Use this in whole group and at literacy stations, too.

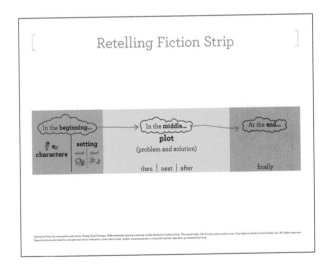

Transitional Readers (Section 4)

Questions to Promote Higher-Level Thinking for Transitional and Fluent Readers are open-ended, thought-provoking questions to use with students in small group to prompt deeper comprehension. Print this list and use it when planning questions to ask students *after* reading in small group. Encourage them to speak in sentences and use new vocabulary from what they read as they discuss the text. You might have students use these questions at Partner Reading stations, too, as they discuss books read together.

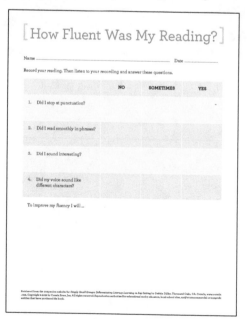

How Fluent Was My Reading? is a kid-friendly fluency reflection tool students can use in small group. Show them the form and point to what to pay attention to (punctuation, phrases, interesting voices, different character voices) as you read a bit. Model how to score yourself and tell why you chose that rating. Print and distribute copies to kids in small group and have them assess their fluency. This can also be used at the Listening and Speaking station.

Sets of **Multiple Meaning Cards** and **Homophone Word Game** cards are provided for vocabulary work with transitional readers. Print two copies of each card available online. Print Multiple Meaning cards on one color of cardstock and Homophone cards on a different color to keep them separate. For each game, turn the cards face down and play the matching game described on page 160. A blank form is included, too, so kids can add their own words to the game. Once children know how to play these games, move the games to the Word Study station.

[Multiple Meaning Cards]		
Print two copies of this page on cardstock. Players take turns finding two words that match.		
bear	brush	change
count	handle	head
leaves	pitcher	pool
shed	stable	train
store	steer	pupil
pound	mine	range

Retrieved from the companion website for *Simply Small Groups: Differentiating Literacy Learning in Any Setting* by Debbie Diller. Thousand Oaks, CA: Corwin, www.corwin.com. Copyright © 2022 by Corwin Press, Inc. All rights reserved. Reproduction authorized for educational use for educators, local school sites, and/or noncommercial or nonprofit entities that have purchased the book.

[Homophone Word Game]		
Print each page on cardstock. Players take turns finding two words that match.		
by	buy	eye
I	hour	our
know	no	knows
nose	mail	male
meet	meat	plain
plane	prints	prince

Reciprocal Teaching Cards can be used to help students improve comprehension. These cards remind readers to use four strategies: predicting, questioning, clarifying, and summarizing the text read. Use these in small group and eventually students may run their groups independently of you.

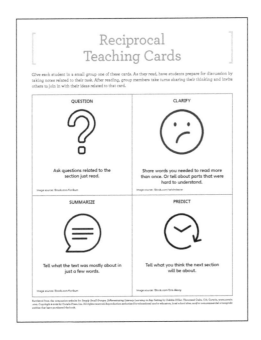

[Reciprocal Teaching Cards]

Give each student in a small group one of these cards. As they read, have students prepare for discussion by taking notes related to their task. After reading, group members take turns sharing their thinking and invite others to join in with their ideas related to that card.

QUESTION — Ask questions related to the section just read.

CLARIFY — Share words you needed to read more than once. Or tell about parts that were hard to understand.

SUMMARIZE — Tell what the text was mostly about in just a few words.

PREDICT — Tell what you think the next section will be about.

Guess the Word for Transitional Readers provides directions with visuals to help children practice reading and writing high-frequency words as a partner game.

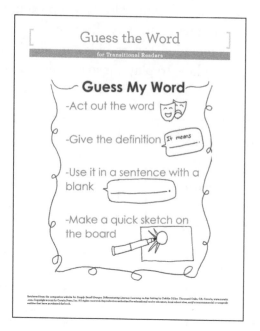

Print and distribute **New Words Bookmarks** to remind students to stop and think about new words and their meanings.

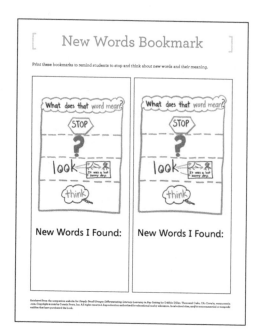

Simply Small Groups

Fluent Readers (Section 5)

Are you using the Lexile or Fountas and Pinnell guided reading levels? Since neither company provides direct correlations between their leveling systems, look at the **Correlation Between Lexile Levels and Guided Reading Levels at the Fluent Stage** chart. It shows approximate ranges you might consider as you select texts for students to use in small groups.

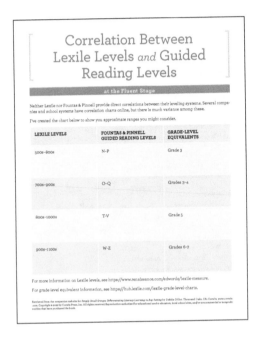

Correlation Between Lexile Levels *and* Guided Reading Levels

at the Fluent Stage

Neither Lexile nor Fountas & Pinnell provide direct correlations between their leveling systems. Several companies and school systems have correlation charts online, but there is much variance among these.

I've created the chart below to show you approximate ranges you might consider.

LEXILE LEVELS	FOUNTAS & PINNELL GUIDED READING LEVELS	GRADE-LEVEL EQUIVALENTS
500s–800s	N–P	Grade 3
700s–900s	O–Q	Grades 3–4
800s–1000s	T–V	Grade 5
900s–1100s	W–Z	Grades 6–7

For more information on Lexile levels, see https://www.renaissance.com/edwords/lexile-measure.

For grade-level equivalent information, see https://hub.lexile.com/lexile-grade-level-charts.

Section 5 details four small group types for fluent readers. Following are some tools for each kind of literacy group. They are all available as printables from the companion website, **resources.corwin.com/simplysmallgroups**.

For guided reading groups, use **Questions to Promote Higher-Level Thinking**. Print this list and use it for planning questions to ask students *after* reading to promote deeper comprehension. Many of these relate to the kinds of questions kids are asked on state reading tests. Adapt the language to include academic vocabulary used in your state standards. Kids can use these same questions at a Partner Reading or Listening and Speaking station.

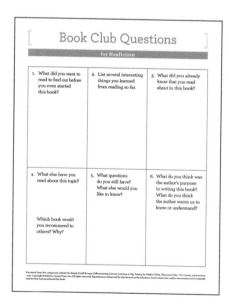

Here are some questions to use when planning for discussion in small groups at the transitional and fluent reading stages.

- Compare _____ to _____ . How were they the same? How were they different?
- What would have happened if _____ ?
- What questions would you ask _____ if you could talk to her?
- Why do you think _____ ?
- What is the theme of this story?
- What makes you think that?
- What is the relationship between _____ and _____ ?
- Suppose you could _____ . What would you do?
- Predict what might happen if _____
- Do you agree with _____ ? Why or why not?
- What is your opinion of _____ ?
- Would it be better if _____ ?
- Why do you think the character _____ ?
- Based on what you know, how would you explain _____ ?
- What would you recommend _____ ?

Book Club Questions are provided for kids to use in preparation for book clubs. You'll find three sheets with open-ended questions and space to write answers. There's one for fiction, one for nonfiction, and another for poetry groups. Cut and paste questions to customize what children might discuss.

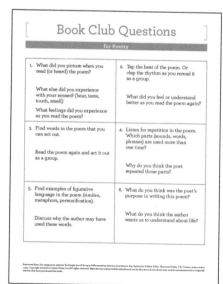

Discussion Leader and **Timekeeper** tags are also included for kids to use during their book club meetings.

For inquiry groups, you'll find **Frayer-a-Friend** and **Frayer-a-Topic** pages. These adaptations of the Frayer model can be used as a starting point to learn about students' interests. Frayer-a-Friend might be used at the beginning of the school year. Use Frayer-a-Topic at the start of a new inquiry to explore an idea.

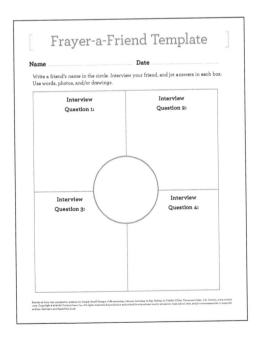

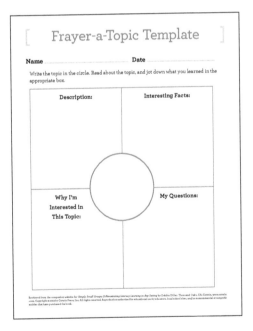

An **Inquiry Chart** is provided for students to take simple notes through words or sketches as they read, view videos, or interview experts. This chart can also be used at an Inquiry station if you have one.

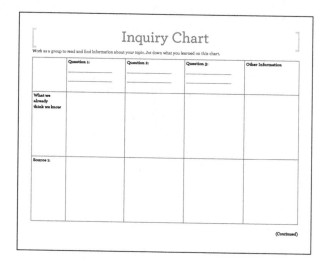

Inquiry Reflection Questions can be used by students to think about their inquiry work. There are questions for students to respond to individually and as a group.

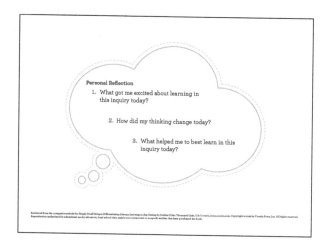

Editor and Author Name Tags are available for students to use when peer editing in writing groups. The editor makes suggestions, and the author makes any changes to what was written. These tags can also be used at a Writing station as kids share their writing with each other.

Writing Focus Board Samples are included for writing groups, too. Use these to help students focus their time and stay on track when meeting as a small group. Feel free to create variations with your students.

Because...
ALL TEACHERS ARE LEADERS

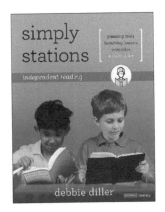

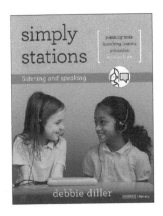

Coming Soon!

Debbie Diller has been refining literacy stations for over 40 years, working with thousands of teachers and students. Her Simply Stations books offer everything you need to plan, teach, and refresh your stations year-round, including

- Step-by-step instructions for launching and maintaining the station;

- Whole group lesson plans, based on key literacy standards, to introduce and support partner work;

- Printable teacher and student tools;

- On-the-spot assessment ideas and troubleshooting tips;

- Lists of grade-level specific materials; and

- Real-classroom photos so you see the possibilities firsthand.

Consulting Available!

If you're interested in consulting, contact Debbie at debbiediller.com

To learn more, visit corwin.com/simplystations

CORWIN

CLN21532

A SAGE Publishing Company